SGT. ROCK's COMBAT TALES

WRITTEN BY
ROBERT KANIGHER

ILLUSTRATED BY
JOE KUBERT
JERRY GRANDENETTI
IRV NOVICK
RUSS HEATH

COLOR RECONSTRUCTION BY
LEE LOUGHRIDGE
DIGITAL CHAMELEON

SGT. ROCK'S COMBAT TALES VOL. 1

Published by DC Comics. Cover and compilation copyright © 2005 DC
Comics. All Rights Reserved. Originally published in single magazine form in
STAR SPANGLED WAR STORIES 72, G.I. COMBAT 56, 68, OUR ARMY AT WAR
83-84, 87-90. Copyright © 1958, 1959, 1960 DC Comics. All Rights
Reserved. All characters, their distinctive likenesses and related elements
featured in this publication are trademarks of DC Comics. The stories,
characters and incidents featured in this publication are entirely fictional.
DC Comics does not read or accept unsolicited submissions of ideas,
stories or artwork. DC Comics, 1700 Broadway, New York, NY 10019.
A Warner Bros. Entertainment Company. Printed in Canada. First Printing.
ISBN: 1-4012-0794-4
Cover illustration by Joe Kubert.
Publication design by John J. Hill.

THEY CALLED HIM THE "HUMAN OBSTACLE COURSE"! YOU HAD TO BEAT HIM--TO BE SOME-ONE! BUT--NO ONE HAD EVER MADE HIM STAY DOWN! NOW--HE WAS FIGHTING IN A DIFFERENT KIND OF RING! WOULD HE STILL BE--

THE ROCK!

"*THE ROCK*" USED TO FIGHT AT THE MAIN STREET ARENA ...

STAY AWAY FROM YOUNG SILK! HIS LEFT IS *DYNAMITE!* LET HIM COME TO YOU! HEAR ME?

I HEAR YOU!

BUT--WHEN THE BELL RANG, "*THE ROCK*" WAS OUT THERE SLUGGING IT OUT WITH THE LATEST MURDEROUS CONTENDER FOR THE CROWN ...

OF COURSE, "*THE ROCK*" WENT DOWN ...

BUT YOU COULDN'T *KEEP* HIM DOWN ...

THAT'S WHY THEY CALLED HIM "*THE ROCK*" ...

C'MON-- AND FIGHT!

SOME MEN ARE GREAT SURGEONS...

OTHERS ARE GREAT PAINTERS..

OTHERS ARE GREAT TEACHERS..

BUT "THE ROCK" WASN'T A GREAT FIGHTER...

HE JUST WOULDN'T STAY DOWN...

SIX... SEVEN... EIGHT... NINE...

THAT WAS ALL HE HAD... SOMETHING IN HIM PUSHED HIM ONTO HIS FEET AGAIN NO MATTER HOW HARD HE HAD BEEN HIT...

C'MON-- AND FIGHT!

EVEN THOUGH HE LOST-- "THE ROCK" ALWAYS ENDED UP ON HIS FEET...

THE WINNER-- ON--POINTS-- YOUNG SILK!

5

"THE ROCK" STOOD IN THE WAY OF EVERY MAN WHO SOUGHT TO CHALLENGE THE CHAMPION...

HE WAS A "HUMAN OBSTACLE COURSE"...

A "HUMAN OBSTACLE COURSE" THAT FIGHTERS HAD TO PASS THROUGH...

TO PROVE THEY WERE ELIGIBLE...

TO MEET THE CHAMP...

BUT WHEN IT WAS OVER... "THE ROCK" WAS ON HIS FEET...

C'MON-- AND FIGHT!

BECAUSE THAT'S ALL HE EVER KNEW...

C'MON-- AND FIGHT!

NOT TO STAY DOWN...

C'MON-- AND FIGHT!

ONCE "THE ROCK" WENT IN AS A SPARRING PARTNER AGAINST THE CHAMP...

HE'LL STAY DOWN WHEN THE *CHAMP* HITS HIM!

NO ONE EVER GETS UP -- WHEN THEY GET HIT LIKE *THAT*!

BUT "THE ROCK" WASN'T "NO ONE"...

HE WAS SOMEONE VERY SPECIAL... *SOMEONE WHO COULDN'T STAY DOWN*...

C'MON-- AND FIGHT!

NO ONE COULD MAKE "THE ROCK" STAY DOWN IN THE RING...

C'MON-- AND FIGHT!

BUT, WAR IS A *DIFFERENT* THING... WAR CAN SHATTER STEEL... WHAT CHANCE WOULD A "HUMAN ROCK" HAVE?

WHAM

BLAM

BAM BAM

"THE ROCK" WAS IN AN ADVANCE OUTPOST THAT HAD JUST COME UNDER ENEMY SHELL FIRE...

2ND BASE CALLING HOME PLATE... COME IN, HOME PLATE! COME IN!

CONCUSSION MUST'VE KNOCKED THE WALKIE-TALKIE OUT OF COMMISSION -- AND THE WHOLE LINE'S DEPENDING ON US FOR NEWS OF THE ENEMY! THIS BARRAGE MAY BE THE SIGNAL FOR AN ENEMY ADVANCE! I'M GOING TO TRY TO GET THROUGH TO OUR LINES!

NO MATTER WHAT HAPPENS -- HOLD THIS PLACE! IF THEY GET THROUGH YOU -- IF THEY KNOCK YOU DOWN -- AND MAYBE YOU STAY DOWN -- THEY'LL SPLIT OUR LINE APART!

STAY ON YOUR FEET -- NO MATTER WHAT!

BLAM

THEY'RE "WALKING" SHELLS IN TOWARD US!

WHROOM

WHAM

BAM

8

THE ENEMY SHELLS "WALKED"...

...RIGHT OVER...

...THE OUTPOST...

BLAM WHAM WHAM BAM BLAM

AND AMIDST THE CORDITE FUMES... AND THE SMOKE FROM THE EXPLOSIONS... ONLY *ONE* FIGURE STARTED TO GROPE TO HIS FEET... UNTIL A ROCK STOOD SWAYING—A "HUMAN ROCK"...

HE TENDED TO THE WOUNDED...

SAVE YOURSELF, JIMMY!

LEAVE US!

"THE ROCK" HAD ONLY *ONE* ANSWER... HE MADE IT AS IF HE HADN'T SEEN A THING... OR HEARD A WORD FROM ANYONE...

C'MON—AND FIGHT!

9

THE ADVANCE ENEMY PATROL DIDN'T EXPECT TO FIND *ANYONE* LEFT IN THE SHELLHOLE ...

BUT *"THE ROCK"* WAS THERE ... WAITING FOR THEM ...

ONE OF THE ENEMY, STARTLED--FELL ...

BUT, THE OTHER TWO CLOSED IN ON *"THE ROCK"* ...

A SKILLFUL JAB-- AND "THE ROCK" WAS DISARMED...

KRAK

A ONE-TWO-- AND "THE ROCK" WAS DOWN..

BUT "THE ROCK" HAD ONE THOUGHT...

I WON'T--STAY DOWN!

... BEATING IN HIM ...

I WON'T STAY DOWN!

... LIKE A GIANT DRUM ...

I WON'T STAY DOWN!

THE FIRST ENEMY NEVER KNEW WHAT HIT HIM ...

THE SECOND ONE DID...

BUT EVEN "A ROCK" CAN GET "DENTED"...

YOU DID ENOUGH!

YOU COULDN'T LIFT A *BULLET* WITH YOUR HANDS!

LOOK AFTER YOUR-SELF!

BUT "THE ROCK" SPOKE AS IF HE HADN'T SEEN A THING... OR HEARD A WORD...

C'MON-- AND FIGHT!

THEN... FOLLOWING BEHIND THE ADVANCE ENEMY PATROL... THE *INEVITABLE* ENEMY TANK...

KLANKETY KLANK KLANK

INCREDULOUSLY, THE WOUNDED MEN WATCHED "THE ROCK"...

SLOWLY... PAINFULLY... WITH USELESS ARMS...

PUSH A ROCKET INTO A BAZOOKA...

12

THEY STARED... STILL UNABLE TO BELIEVE WHAT THEY SAW... THEY SAW HIM DRAG THE HEAVY BAZOOKA AFTER HIM...

HE SHOULDN'T HAVE BEEN ABLE TO EVEN *CRAWL*-- BUT-- *"THE ROCK"* STOOD UP...

C'MON-- AND FIGHT!

THE *TANK* SAW THE LONE FIGURE... AND SWUNG ITS *MACHINE GUNS* AT IT... LIKE GLOVES OF STEEL...

RATATAT

TZINNNG

ZING

BEEOW

BWEEEEEE

SOMEHOW... *"THE ROCK"* STOOD THERE... A SINGLE *T.N.T.* PUNCH IN ITS FIST...

C'MON-- AND FIGHT!

NOW, THE TANK UNLEASHED ITS HEAVY PUNCH...

BAM

"*THE ROCK*" TOPPLED--AS HE HAD SO OFTEN IN THE PAST...

AND THEN ... BECAUSE HE KNEW ONLY *ONE THING*-- THAT HE COULDN'T STAY DOWN...

HE ROSE ...

IT SEEMED TO TAKE A *MILLION YEARS* FOR HIM TO LIFT THE BAZOOKA TO HIS SHOULDER...

AND *ANOTHER* MILLION TO FIRE ...

WHOOSH

BUT IT ONLY TOOK AN *INSTANT* FOR THE ROCKET TO BURY ITSELF IN THE TANK'S AMMO...

BLANG

WHREEEEEEEE

MEN WHO COULDN'T RISE -- ROSE TO THEIR FEET... MEN WHO COULDN'T LIFT A FINGER -- LIFTED RIFLES... MEN WHO COULDN'T FIGHT ... FOUGHT...

ALL BECAUSE OF "*THE ROCK*"... WHO KNEW ONLY *ONE* THING... HE *COULDN'T* STAY DOWN...

The End

THE FIRST MAN WHO "GREETED" US ON THE ISLAND WAS OUR DRILL INSTRUCTOR...

WHEN THEY TOLD ME TO MAKE MARINES OF YOU CHARACTERS--THEY DIDN'T SEE WHAT YOU LOOK LIKE! I HAVE--AND I SAY IT'S IMPOSSIBLE!

WE "HEARD" HIM DURING THE NIGHT TOO...

YOU JOKERS COULDN'T EVEN SPELL MARINES! THEY MADE A MISTAKE ISSUIN' YOU RIFLES! WHOEVER HEARD OF SAND FLEAS FIRIN' RIFLES?

WE TRAMPED OUR BOOTS OFF TRYING TO KEEP UP WITH THE PACE HE SET ON HIKES...WE ATE HIS DUST FOR HUNDREDS OF MILES... BUT WE NEVER CAUGHT UP TO THE D.I.!

YOU SAND FLEAS STUCK IN OLLIE OR SOMETHIN'?

HARRUP TWO-THREE-FOUR!

HARRUPTWO--

AND WHEN I WAS GALLOPING AFTER MY BREATH DURING A TWO-MINUTE BREAK-- MY RIFLE WAS SUDDENLY RIPPED OUT OF MY HANDS...

WHA-?

I GOT IT BACK ALL RIGHT...

YOU HELD THAT RIFLE AS IF IT WAS A BABY'S RATTLE! IF I WAS THE ENEMY YOU'D NEVER SEE IT AGAIN! HOLD IT SO TIGHT IT BECOMES A PART OF YOUR ARM!

WHACK

WE WENT THROUGH COMBAT TRAINING WHEN RAIN HAD TURNED THE AREA INTO A SEA OF *MUD*...

FLATTEN OUT, YOU *SAND FLEAS!* THAT'S NOT *CONFETTI*-- THAT'S *STEEL* FLYIN' AROUND!

WHOMP

AS THE *MACHINE GUNS* WHIP-LASHED OVER US--A HAND SLAMMED THE BACK OF MY HELMET...

BEEEOW

DON'T BE AFRAID OF THE MUD, *SAND FLEA*-- IT'LL MAKE YOU *PRETTY!*

SQUOOSH

BEEOW

TZNNNG

OUR *MACHINE GUNS* ARE FIRIN' FROM *FIXED MOUNTS!* BUT THE *ENEMY* PLAYS FOR *KEEPS!* IF YOU DON'T KEEP YOUR HEAD *DOWN*-- YOU WON'T KEEP IT *ON* FOR *LONG!* CATCH?

TZNG

JUST LOOKING AT THE BACK OF HIS HEAD MADE OUR BLOOD BOIL...

I CATCH!

THE *D.I.* MADE US DO EVERY-THING IN DOUBLE-TIME -- EVEN "RELAXING"...

RELAX, *SAND FLEA!* WHEN I TELL YOU TO RELAX-- R...E...L...A...X...-- RE-LAX!

7

I "RELAXED" UNTIL MY BACK--ARMS AND LEGS-- SEEMED TO SNAP IN TWO...

LINE YOUR SIGHTS HOLD YOUR BREATH SQUEEZE YOUR TRIGGER SQUEEZE SQUEEZESQUEEZE!

K-POW

WHAT D'YA KNOW, *SAND FLEA!* THE WIND CARRIED YOUR BULLET SMACK *INTO* THE BULL'S-EYE!

THE D.I. WAS ON OUR BACKS BY DAY...

SPREAD OUT, YOU SAND FLEAS! OR ONE SHELL'LL SPREAD YOU ALL OUT!

WHUMP

DANGER EXPL. AREA

AND BY NIGHT...

C'MON, YOU SAND FLEAS! YOU DON'T NEED ANY LIGHT TO ASSEMBLE YOUR RIFLES! DO YOU THINK THE ENEMY'LL WAIT UNTIL DAYLIGHT IN CASE YOU HAVE TO FIX A JAM IN THE DARK?

AND WHILE I WAS WAITING FOR THE D.I. TO INSPECT MY RIFLE...

STILL HOLDIN' YOUR RIFLE AS IF IT WAS A BABY'S RATTLE! DO YOU THINK THE ENEMY'LL BLOW A BUGLE BEFORE THEY TRY TO DISARM YOU?

TRY TO HOLD ONTO IT, SAND FLEA! IF YOU THINK IT'S TOO HEAVY TO CARRY--MAYBE WE'LL ISSUE YOU A BROOM! CATCH?

SMACK

I CATCH!

ON THE GRENADE-THROWING RANGE LATER..

DON'T THROW THAT POTATO YET, SAND FLEA!

GRENADE

DON'T THROW A GRENADE UNTIL IT'S *TOO HOT* FOR THE ENEMY TO TOSS IT *BACK* IN YOUR LAP!

HOLD IT!

HOLD IT!

NOW!

LET IT COOK UNTIL IT EXPLODES ON *CONTACT*--AND THE ENEMY WILL NEVER BE ABLE TO GIVE *YOU* A HOT FOOT WITH YOUR *OWN* GRENADE! REMEMBER--YOU'RE A *SAND FLEA*--YOU BRUISE *EASILY!* CATCH?

BLAM

I CATCH!

BUT NONE OF US COULD EVER *CATCH UP* TO HIM NO MATTER HOW HARD WE TRIED-- NO MATTER WHAT PROBLEM WE WERE TACKLING...

HE'S AHEAD OF US AGAIN! C'MON-- C'MON!

SOMEHOW THE *D.I.* WANGLED HIMSELF A TRANSFER TO OUR OUTFIT WHEN WE SHIPPED OUT... AND WHEN WE WENT DOWN THE LANDING NETS...

C'MON DOWN THOSE NETS, SAND FLEAS! YOU CAN *STOP* FOR REFRESHMENTS *LATER!*

DURING THE ENTIRE RIDE TO THE BEACH WE WERE UNDER HEAVY ATTACK...

BLAM WHAM

WHAM

WHUMB

BUT NO ONE BLINKED AN EYELASH--BECAUSE ALL *WE* HEARD...

WHAM

THEY SENT *ME* ALONG TO NURSE YOU--IN CASE YOU STUB YOUR TOES OR SOMETHIN'! SO STAY *CLOSE* TO ME AND I'LL TAKE GOOD CARE OF YOU! *CATCH,* SAND FLEAS?

WHEN THE RAMP WENT DOWN, WE ALL SHOT OUT LIKE ROCKETS FROM BAZOOKAS...

CATCH!

WE'RE NOTHIN' BUT *SAND FLEAS* IF WE EAT HIS DUST AGAIN! C'MON-- LET'S GO--*LET'S GO!*

BEOW   TING   ZIP   TING

END OF PART I

21

WE RAN RIGHT INTO THE ENEMY ARTILLERY SIGHTS... BUT EVEN ABOVE THE SOUND OF THE EXPLODING SHELLS--WE *STILL* HEARD THE *D.I.* SHOUTING...

SPREAD OUT, YOU SAND FLEAS!-- OR *ONE* SHELL'LL SPREAD YOU *ALL* OUT!

BLAM

WE HEARD THE *D.I.'s* VOICE JUST BEFORE THE NEXT SHELL SLAMMED THE SKY AND THE GROUND TOGETHER...

SPREAD OUT!

WHAM

WE HIT THE GROUND AS A *MACHINE GUN* OPENED UP ON US...

FLATTEN!

BEEOW

ZIP TZUNG

ZIP ZINNG BWEE

WE CRAWLED FORWARD IN THE DIRECTION OF THE FIRING...

FLATTEN OUT-- OR YOU'LL HEAR HIM YELLING-- "THAT'S NOT CONFETTI, SAND FLEAS--THAT'S STEEL FLYIN' AROUND!"

PTWEEE

TZ'INNNG

BEEOW

THE ENEMY SEARCHED FOR US WITH FINGERS OF LEAD...

TAKKATAKKA

BUT ABOVE THE HAMMERING OF THE MACHINE GUN WE HEARD ONLY *ONE* SOUND--*HIS* VOICE!

IF YOU DON'T KEEP YOUR HEADS *DOWN*-- YOU WON'T HAVE IT *ON* FOR *LONG!* CATCH?

B^WEEE

TZ'NNG

BEEOW

TZ'NNG

CATCH!

BY THIS TIME, WE WERE ALMOST WITHIN GRENADE RANGE OF THE *MACHINE GUN*... I PULLED THE PIN...

TZ'NNG

BEEOW

...LET THE PRIMER SPRING CLEAR...

PLING

BUT JUST AS I WAS ABOUT TO HEAVE IT...

DON'T TOSS A GRENADE UNLESS IT'S *TOO HOT* FOR THE ENEMY TO TOSS *BACK* IN YOUR LAP!

TZ'NNG

BWEE

Z'P

BEEOW

THE ENEMY GUNNERS SPOTTED ME AND CONCENTRATED THEIR FIRE ON ME...

TAKKA TAKKA

BUT ALL *I* HEARD WAS THE D.I.'s VOICE...

HOLD IT!

Z'P Z'P TZINNG

THE *MACHINE GUN* TRIED TO SLAM THE GRENADE OUT OF MY HAND...

TAKKA TAKKA

WHILE I COUNTED OFF THE SECONDS...

HOLD IT!

WHEEE

THEN...

NOW!

WHAM

AS WE SLOGGED PAST THE KAYOED M.G. NEST...

C'MON! THE D.I. CAN'T BE *TOO* FAR AHEAD OF US!

YEAH! WE'VE GOT TO CATCH UP TO HIM BEFORE HE TELLS US WHAT *SAND FLEAS* WE ARE!

BUT...

WHERE IS HE?

KNOCKING OUT *YARDS* TO OUR *INCHES*-- AS USUAL! C'MON! DOUBLE-TIME UNTIL WE LEAP-FROG OVER HIM!

WE HAD REACHED THE SANDY BEACH OF A RIVER WITHOUT SPOTTING THE *D.I.* -- BUT THE ENEMY *HOWITZER* DUG IN ON THE OTHER SIDE SPOTTED *US...*

BLAM

THE SHELL CUT TREES DOWN ALL AROUND US... AND SENT WAVES OF STINGING SAND AT US...

WHAM

HIT THE DECK!

RRRIP

WE CAN'T REACH THEM WITH GRENADES! OUR ONLY CHANCE IS *RIFLE FIRE!* WE'LL BE HIT IF WE FIRE *STANDING!* THE GROUND'S SHAKING TOO MUCH FOR *KNEELING* OR *PRONE* FIRE! SITTING POSITION WILL BE THE MOST ACCURATE!

BAM

ABOVE THE EXPLODING *HOWITZER* SHELLS I HEARD...

RELAX, SAND FLEA! LINE UP YOUR SIGHT HOLD-YOUR BREATH SQUEEZE-YOUR TRIGGER SQUEEZE-SQUEEZE SQUEEZE--!

POW POW

POW POW

KPOW POW

POW POW

KPOW POW POW POW

BUT WE DIDN'T HAVE A CHANCE TO RELAX FOR LONG...

ENEMY INFANTRY HITTING US FROM THE *SIDE* -- WHILE *WE* WERE CONCENTRATING ON KNOCKING OUT THE *MORTAR!*

THE ENEMY TORE INTO US AS IF THEY EXPECTED TO TRAMPLE RIGHT OVER US -- BUT -- *WE STOOD FIRM...*

BANZAI BANZAI

C'MON, SAND FLEAS! YOU STUCK IN *GLUE* OR SOMETHIN'?

THEN *WE* SLAMMED FORWARD...

THE *D.I.* WONDERS WHAT MAKES US *SAND FLEAS* THINK WE COULD MAKE *MARINES* ? *LET'S SHOW HIM!*

SUDDENLY, IT WAS SILENT... SO SILENT...

WE NEVER SAW HIM AGAIN ONCE WE STARTED OVER THAT DUNE ON THE BEACH!

HE'S NOT HERE!

WE NEVER REALLY HEARD HIM, EITHER!

THEY CLAPPED US ON THE BACK AND LET US RETURN TO THE BEACH TO LOOK FOR THE *D.I.* ... WE FOUND HIM *STILL ON THE OTHER SIDE OF THE DUNE* ...

IF IT WASN'T FOR *YOU* -- WE *NEVER* COULD HAVE DONE IT!

WE'RE MARINES *NOW*, AREN'T WE ?

YOU *STILL* HOLD THAT RIFLE AS IF IT WAS A *BABY'S RATTLE!*

THAT'S BECAUSE YOU'RE *STILL A SAND FLEA!* BUT, MAYBE I *CAN* MAKE *MARINES* OF *YOU* -- IF THE WAR LASTS *LONG* ENOUGH!

The End

WHEREVER THE FIGHTING MEN GO ABOUT THEIR BUSINESS... NO MATTER WHERE THEY ARE... IN THE FOXHOLES...

WHAM

HEAR THE LATEST ABOUT EASY COMPANY?

WHO HASN'T?

IN THE AIR...

HEAR THE LATEST ABOUT "THE ROCK" OF EASY COMPANY?

YOU MEAN SGT. ROCK?

WHAM

RATATAT

ON THE SEA...

HEAR THE LATEST ABOUT EASY COMPANY?

WHUMP
WHUMP
WHUMP
WHUMP

OR UNDER IT...

HEAR THE LATEST ABOUT EASY COMPANY?

YOU MEAN WHAT HAPPENED WHEN SGT. ROCK MET...?

YES, THE STORIES ABOUT EASY COMPANY KEPT FIGHTING MEN WARM ON EVERY FRONT...

WONDER WHY THEY CALL US EASY COMPANY?

YEAH-- NOTHIN' EVER COMES EASY TO US!

KPOW POW

RATATAT

VOOMP

VOOMP

AND THE ONE MAN IN EASY WHO WAS MOST TALKED ABOUT, WAS ITS "ROCK"... SGT. ROCK...

C'MON, CHICKENS! YOU CAN SET AFTER THE WAR IS OVER!

BAM

29

EASY COMPANY WAS ALMOST CONTINUALLY ON THE LINE ...SO A STEADY STREAM OF REPLACEMENTS WAS NEEDED TO KEEP IT UP TO FIGHTING STRENGTH...

TAKE CARE OF THESE PIGEONS, GUYS!

OKAY, ROCK!

WHY D'YA CALL THE SARGE "ROCK"?

'CAUSE THAT'S WHAT HE IS! 'CAUSE WHEN THE GOIN' GETS SO RUGGED THAT ONLY A ROCK COULD STAND...

... HE STANDS!

ONE DAY, A NEW REPLACEMENT CAME INTO EASY COMPANY-- A BIG TOUGH VET WHO HAD BEEN SEPARATED FROM HIS OUTFIT...

THAT WAS CLOSE!

NOT CLOSE ENOUGH TO NICK JOE WALL!

TZING   ZIP   VIP
TZINNG   ZIP   ZING
ZIP

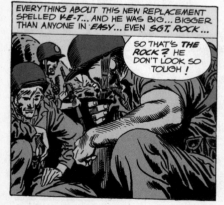

EVERYTHING ABOUT THIS NEW REPLACEMENT SPELLED V-E-T... AND HE WAS BIG... BIGGER THAN ANYONE IN EASY... EVEN SGT. ROCK...

SO THAT'S THE ROCK? HE DON'T LOOK SO TOUGH!

IF THE ROCK HEARD... HE DIDN'T ANSWER...

THE ENEMY WAS TOUGH... THEY ADVANCED BEHIND A TANK TO MAKE IT EVEN TOUGHER FOR EASY CO. ...

THIS TIME WE SWEEP THE AMERIKANER COMPANY BACK INTO THE SEA!

KLANKETY-KLANK

EASY'S FORWARD LINE PEERED OVER ITS SLIT TRENCH..

CAN'T LIFT YOUR HEAD UP TO GET A LOOK AT WHAT'S COMIN'-- WITHOUT GETTIN' IT SHAVED BY THAT MACHINE GUN! WE'LL STAY PUT UNTIL THEY COME AT US--THEN BLAST 'EM!

BWEEOW

RATATATAT

TZING

ZZING

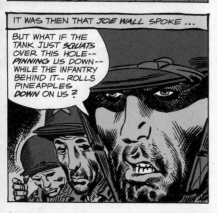

IT WAS THEN THAT JOE WALL SPOKE ...

BUT WHAT IF THE TANK JUST SQUATS OVER THIS HOLE-- PINNING US DOWN-- WHILE THE INFANTRY BEHIND IT-- ROLLS PINEAPPLES DOWN ON US ?

IF WE STOP THE TANK-- THE INFANTRY WILL LOSE ITS ROLLING COVER! GIVE ME SOME RAPID FIRE! I'M GOING OUT!

Z'INNNG

BEEEOW

TZING

ZINNNG

THE MEN OF EASY IGNORED THE HAIL OF FIRE COMING AT THEM--AND COVERED JOE WALL AS HE CRAWLED TOWARDS THE ONCOMING TANK ...

POW

RATATATATAT

KPOW

KPOW

POW

ZING

TZING

ZP

THE NEW MAN COOLLY LAY IN THE PATH OF THE ONCOMING *TANK* AND PRIMED A FEW GRENADES...

THE ENEMY *DOGFEET* BEHIND THE *TANK* CAN'T FIRE AT ME-- WITHOUT EXPOSING THEMSELVES TO MY COVER FIRE!

SO IT'S BETWEEN THE *TANK* AND *ME*!

THE MEN OF *EASY* WATCHED THE MAN WHO WAS TACKLING THE *TANK* OUT FRONT...

LOOK AT HIM LAY THERE-- WITH THAT TANK COMIN' ON--AS IF NOTHIN' CAN MOVE HIM!

HE'S LIKE A *WALL*!

KPOW POW KPOW POW POW BUDDABUDDA POW

UNDER THE TANK'S ANGLE OF FIRE... *JOE WALL* WAITED AS THE STEEL MASS LOOMED OVER HIM...

HERE GOES A DOUBLE HOT-FOOT!

PLING PLING

THOSE CHARACTERS IN BACK OF THE TANK WILL BE WAITING FOR IT TO CLEAR ME--

KLANKETY KLANK KLANK

SO THEY CAN JUMP ME--

SO I'LL PLAY DEAD!

AND AS THE TANK GROUND ON TOWARD *EASY*... THE ENEMY SAW THE PRONE FIGURE ON THE GROUND...

LOOK-- OUR TANK GOT THE FOOL!

MAYBE NOT--

KLANK

KLANKETY KLANK

WE MUST MAKE SURE!

*I*T WAS AT THAT MOMENT THAT THE GRENADES STUCK IN-SIDE THE TANK TREADS EXPLODED...

BLAM BAM BAM

AND WHILE THE ENEMY WAS MOMENTARILY STARTLED...JOE WALL SEIZED THE RIFLE MUZZLE AND...

GIVE ME THIS FLY SWATTER!

POW

*A*ND EVEN WHILE THE MEN OF *EASY* ATTACKED THE STALLED *TANK* AND STREAMED TOWARDS THE ENEMY INFANTRY... THEIR EYES WERE FIXED UPON A LONE FIGURE...WHO STOOD IMMOVABLE AS A *WALL*!

33

WHREEEEEEEEEEE

IT WAS SGT. ROCK, THE "ROCK" OF EASY CO., WHO PUT THE FINISHING TOUCHES TO THE ENEMY TANK...

SCATTER!

BLANG

BUT THE MEN'S EYES WERE UPON THE TOUGH NEW REPLACEMENT WHO WAS A BIG MAN IN EVERY WAY...

DID YOU SEE THAT JOE WALL? THE ENEMY COULDN'T CLIMB OVER HIM!

SGT. ROCK'S THE "ROCK" OF EASY!

AND THIS GUY'S THE "WALL"!

AND THE NEWLY NICKNAMED THE "WALL" OF EASY GLANCED AT THE "ROCK" OF EASY...

SO THAT'S THE ROCK, HUH? HE DON'T LOOK SO TOUGH!

BUT IF THE ROCK OF EASY CO. HEARD... HE DIDN'T ANSWER...

THAT *FORT'S* IN TROUBLE-- IT NEEDS HELP!

*T*HEN CAME THE DAY WHEN A FLYING FORT MADE A FORCED LANDING IN FRONT OF THE GROUND HELD BY *EASY CO...*

SPUT-SPUTTER-SPUT

AS THE MEN OF *EASY* STARTED FORWARD FOR THE BATTERED PLANE...

MORTAR FIRE!

BAM BLAM BAM WHAM

THE *ROCK* OF *EASY* CO. WAVED THE MEN BACK...

THOSE CUTE CHARACTERS ON THE OTHER SIDE KNOW WE'RE GOING TO TRY TO HELP THE *FORT*--SO THEY'RE ZEROING IN ON US --GET BACK! GET BACK! THEY MIGHT *EVEN* SPRING A COUNTER-- ATTACK ON US!

EVEN WHILE THE MEN FELL BACK, THE *ROCK* RAN ON...

THEY'RE NOT BLASTING THE SHIP! PROBABLY GOING TO HAVE A TRY AT CAPTURING IT THEM- SELVES --FOR THE BOMB SIGHT...

BLAM

*S*UDDENLY, THE *ROCK* REALIZED THAT DESPITE THE RAIN OF MORTAR SHELLS AROUND HIM--HE WAS *NOT ALONE...*

THOUGHT I TOLD YOU TO GO BACK?

WHAAT ?... CAN'T HEAR A THING WITH ALL THESE EGGSHELLS BEING TOSSED AT US!

WHAM

BAM

JUST AS THE TWO MEN REACHED THE GROUNDED *FORT*... THE PILOT HAILED THEM...

SHIP'S FIXED... READY TO GO UP AGAIN... BUT WE'VE NO MEN LEFT TO MAN OUR GUNS--AND WE'VE STILL GOT AN A-1 TARGET TO HIT!

MISTER--I DON'T KNOW ABOUT THE SARGE HERE--BUT GUNS IS MY MIDDLE NAME!

THE *ROCK OF EASY CO.* DIDN'T SAY ANYTHING AS HE AND THE *WALL* SCRAMBLED TO THEIR GUN POSITIONS IN THE WAIST...

YOU LOOK A LITTLE SMALL BEHIND THAT FIFTY, SARGE -- BUT IT'S JUST MY SIZE!

THE ENEMY HAD SENT AN ARMORED CAR OUT TO STOP THE FORT... BUT THE CAR RAN INTO A WALL OF .50 SLUGS...

YOU MIGHT AS WELL GRAB YOURSELF SOME SHUTEYE, SARGE--I'LL TAKE CARE OF ANY TARGETS!

RATATA-WHAM

THE *ROCK* DIDN'T SAY ANYTHING AS HE LOOKED DOWN A HALF HOUR LATER... AT THE TARGET THE PILOT HAD TOLD THEM THEY WERE GOING TO ATTACK AT LOW LEVEL...

A ROCKET LAUNCHING PLATFORM...

WHUMP

WHUMP

HE DIDN'T HAVE TO SAY ANYTHING TO THE *WALL*...AS THE ENEMY FIGHTERS BORE IN...

JUST SHOO THESE CHICKENS AROUND TO *MY* SIDE, SARGE--I'LL TAKE CARE OF 'EM!

RATATA

SUDDENLY, THE *WALL* WAS HIT...

CAN'T--LIFT MY ARMS-- TO--FIRE--! GOT TO-- GOT TO--BUT I-- CAN'T--! AND A FIGHTER-- IS COMING--THIS WAY--!

TZINNG

Z'NG

THE ROCK DIDN'T SAY ANYTHING AS HE SPRANG TO THE *WALL'S* FIFTY AND TRACKED THE ENEMY FIGHTER...

RATATAT

THE *ROCK* DIDN'T SAY A WORD AS HE WENT FROM GUN...

WHY CAN'T-- I HELP?

RATATA

TO GUN...

WHAT KIND OF A SOLDIER AM I?

TO GUN...

WHAT GOOD AM I?

TATAT

AND THEN... WHEN THE TARGET HAD BEEN HIT... AND THE LAST FIGHTER WAS BORING IN FOR THE KILL ... *THE ROCK* DIDN'T SAY ANYTHING AS HE HELPED *THE WALL* TO HIS GUN ...

ZING ZIP

ZIP

HE STILL DIDN'T SAY ANYTHING AS HE PLACED *THE WALL* INTO POSITION BEHIND HIS *FIFTY*...

YOU'RE HELPING ME--FIRE-- MY--GUN--!

RATAT

IF THE ENEMY FIGHTER THOUGHT IT HAD AN EASY TARGET... IT DIDN'T KNOW THAT THE MEN BEHIND THE TARGET CAME FROM *EASY*... WHERE THE FIGHTING IS *NEVER* EASY...

WE GOT IT--*WE GOT IT*--BUT ONLY BECAUSE *YOU* DIDN'T BUDGE!

RATATAT

WHAM

WEEKS LATER... WHEN EVERYONE KNEW ABOUT WHAT HAD HAPPENED... NEW REPLACEMENTS CAME UP TO *EASY* AS USUAL...

WHY DO THEY CALL HIM THE *ROCK OF EASY?*

BECAUSE A *WALL* MAY FALL, BUSTER--

IT'S *EASY* HERE!

--BUT NOT A *ROCK!*

The End

It was the strangest situation of the war! **Easy Company** had been ordered to leave their foxholes -- before a massive enemy attack steamrollered over them!
But they not only ignored the order -- they laughed! Here is the amazing story of **Easy Company** and their ...

LAUGHTER ON SNAKEHEAD HILL!

As *SGT. ROCK* of *EASY CO.* LED HIS BATTLE—HARDENED MEN UP THE FROZEN GROUND OF *SNAKEHEAD HILL* ...

C'MON CHICKENS! IF WE DON'T GET INTO POSITION BEFORE THE SUN RISES--WE'LL BE A PRETTY SIGHT FOR THE ENEMY GUNNERS!

OKAY! HERE'S WHERE WE SET UP HOUSE! *DIG!*

SARGE! THE GROUND'S LIKE ROCK! OUR SHOVELS CAN'T EVEN RAISE A LITTLE POWDER!

WHAT'LL WE USE FOR COVER, SARGE--WHEN THE SUN RISES?

CHUNK!

THE "*ROCK*" OF *EASY CO.* LOOKED IN THE DIRECTION OF THE HIDDEN ENEMY...

GUESS WE'LL HAVE TO LEAVE IT TO THOSE BUZZARDS UP THERE! IF WE HANG ON--*THEY'LL* GIVE US COVER!

MEANWHILE, ABOVE IN THE ENEMY-HELD POSITIONS ON *SNAKEHEAD HILL* ...

THE AMERIKANERS ARE MOVING INTO POSITION BELOW US! I DON'T HAVE TO SEE THEM! I'LL LET THEM MAKE THEMSELVES COMFORTABLE--THEN OPEN MY BAG OF SURPRISES FOR THEM!

ON **SNAKEHEAD HILL** BELOW THE ENEMY-- **SGT. ROCK** AND THE MEN OF **EASY** WAITED FOR THE SUN TO RISE ...

I FEEL LIKE A FLY STUCK IN MOLASSES!

STOP YOUR BUZZIN', MISTER FLY!

THE MEN OF **EASY** LAUGHED WITHOUT MAKING A SOUND...AND WAITED...

THE ENEMY OFFICER WAITED TOO...

THE AMERIKANERS MUST BE SWEPT OFF THE HILL --OR WE WILL LOSE THE RIDGE-- **THE EYE** THAT DIRECTS OUR ARTILLERY AT THE AMERIKANER ARMY'S EVERY MOVE!

THE ENEMY MACHINE GUN CREWS DUG IN IN SOLID ROCK WAITED TOO FOR THE SUN TO RISE..

SO DID THE ENEMY MORTARS PLACED FOR HIGH ANGLE FIRE IN GULLEYS AND RAVINES ON THE OTHER SIDE OF THE RIDGE ...

THE ENEMY IN TANK TURRETS SLUNK AND MADE INTO IMPENE-TRABLE PILL-BOXES ON THE RIDGE...WAITED TOO..

41

THE SUN ROSE LIKE A GREAT BEAM ...

FOCUSED ON THE MEN OF *EASY* ON *SNAKEHEAD HILL*...

LYING ON **TOP** OF THE FLINT-LIKE GROUND...

AND THE ENEMY OFFICER SMILED... AND GAVE HIS ORDER ...

FIRE!

FIRST THE ENEMY MACHINE GUNS FIRED DOWN FIRE LANES THAT THEY HAD MEMORIZED IN THEIR SLEEP...

RATATATA

RATATATAT

THEN THE SUNKEN TANK TURRETS WITH THEIR DREADED *88s*..

BAM!

BAM!

BAM!

THEN THE MORTARS WHIRLED OUT SEARCHING FOR THE MEN OF *EASY*...

WHUMP!

WHUMP!

42

ON *SNAKEHEAD HILL*, THE ENEMY OFFICER ORDERED THE FIRE TO LIFT TO CUT OFF THE MEN OF *EASY* FROM ANY REINFORCEMENTS ...

INFANTRY--FORWARD! WHILE THE AMERIKANERS ARE TOO DAZED TO FIGHT BACK!

THE ENEMY'S ELITE CORPS--ALL BATTLE-HARDENED VETS--MOVED CONFIDENTLY DOWN THE SLOPE TOWARDS THE *G.I.s*...PROTECTED BY COVER FIRE ...

WE SHALL BE ON TOP OF THEM--BEFORE THEY DARE LIFT THEIR HEADS! THEN WE WILL SWEEP THEM OFF THE HILL!

BAM! BLAM! WHAM!

SGT. ROCK OF EASY CO. WATCHED THE ENEMY SHELLFIRE ...

IT'S LIFTIN'! THAT MUST MEAN THEIR INFANTRY IS RIGHT BEHIND IT!

WHROOM! WHEEEE!

DON'T OPEN FIRE! IF YOU DO--THEY'LL CALL FOR ARTILLERY FIRE AGAIN! LET 'EM COME SO CLOSE TO US--THAT THEY'LL BE AFRAID TO USE COVER FIRE FOR FEAR OF HITTIN' THEIR OWN MEN!

BEHIND HIS LITTLE BARRICADE OF LOOSE ROCKS, *SGT. ROCK OF EASY CO.* LAY SPRAWLED AS ENEMY BOOTS CLOMPED TOWARDS HIM ...

IF THEY THINK I'M ONLY PLAYIN' DEAD--THEY'LL MAKE IT PERMANENT!

THIS BUZZARD'S STOPPIN'! HE'S BEEN AROUND BEFORE! HE'S SEEN THIS ACT!

SILENTLY, **SGT. ROCK** PULLED THE ENEMY DOWN TOWARD HIM ...

KROW!

YOU'RE NOT RETIRIN' **THIS** ACT, **BUZZARD**! YOU'RE THE ONE THAT'S REACHED THE RETIREMENT AGE!

IMMEDIATELY, THE **ROCK** WAS SURROUNDED BY A WAVE OF THE ENEMY...

IF THEY WEREN'T TOO CLOSE TO FIRE--

--THEY'D PICK ME OFF--

--AS IF I WAS A FLY ON A PIE!

THE MEN OF EASY LEFT THEIR SHELL-BLASTED HOLES AND MET THE ENEMY HEAD-ON LIKE HUMAN BATTERING RAMS...

C'MON, **EASY**!

YEAH--WE CAN'T LET THE **ROCK** DO IT ALL BY HIM-SELF!

THE ENEMY FELL BACK--BUT NOW THERE WAS MORE ROOM IN THE SHELL-BLASTED HOLES IN THE ROCKY GROUND OF *SNAKEHEAD HILL* ...

KEEP YOUR HEADS DOWN, CHICKS! WE'RE DUE FOR ANOTHER PASTIN'!

YEAH--THE BOSS OF THE BUZZARDS ON THE RIDGE WON'T LIKE THE WAY WE PLAY!

ON THE RIDGE, THE ENEMY LOOKED DOWN ON *EASY COMPANY* AND..

CONCENTRATED FIRE! FIRE! FIRE!

ENEMY MACHINE GUNS--MORTARS--AND SUNKEN TANKS POURED FIRE DOWN ON THE MEN OF *EASY* CLINGING TO THEIR POSITION ON THE HILL ..

WHUMP! WHUMP! BAM! BAM! BAM!

RAT-A-TA-TA-RATA TA-TA!

WHEN THE FIRE LIFTED--THE ENEMY ATTACKED--AND THE *MEN OF EASY* FOUGHT BACK ... WHILE THE SUN AND THE RAIN AND THE SNOW BEAT DOWN ON THEM ...

POW! K-POW!

POW! POW!

POW! BRATATATATAT!

TIME CEASED TO EXIST FOR THE MEN OF *EASY*...

HEY, ROCK! WHAT NUMBER ATTACK IS THIS ONE?

WHO'S COUNTIN'?

POW! *KPOW!*

AND SOMETHING STRANGE BE-GAN HAPPENING TO THEM ...

ROCK--LOOK! I CAN'T LET GO OF MY RIFLE! I'VE BEEN SQUEEZIN' IT SO LONG--*I CAN'T LET GO OF IT!*

ME TOO!

YOU CHICKS ARE GETTIN' COMBAT-- HAPPY!

POW!

BUT AS HE FIRED INTO ANOTHER ENEMY ATTACK, THE *ROCK* KNEW..

I FOUND THAT OUT A COUPLE OF DAYS AGO!

POW!

KPOW!

DAY AFTER DAY, THE BATTERED REMNANTS OF *EASY* HELD FAST AGAINST WITHERING FIRE AND ENEMY ATTACKS -- *UNTIL* ...

JAWOHL! I WILL LEAD THE NEXT ATTACK IN FORCE -- *PERSONALLY* -- AND SWEEP THOSE MISERABLE INSECTS OFF THE HILL!

MEANWHILE, STARTING UP THE BOTTOM OF *SNAKEHEAD HILL* --A FRESH COMPANY OF G.I.s...

H.Q. REPORTS ENEMY ON RIDGE MASSING FOR A BIG ATTACK AGAINST EASY! EASY DID THE IMPOSSIBLE -- HOLDING ON *THIS* LONG! WE'VE GOT TO RELIEVE THEM BEFORE THE ATTACK STARTS -- OR THE ENEMY WILL ROLL RIGHT OVER THEM!

AND WE'LL BE CAUGHT TOO, SIR! SURE -- WE'VE GOT TO TAKE OVER *EASY'S* POSITIONS UP THERE!

THE NEW COMPANY GOT WITHIN HAILING DISTANCE OF *EASY* WHEN A CURTAIN OF FIRE DROPPED DOWN..

WHAM! *BLAM!*

THEY'RE CUTTING US OFF FROM EASY!

BAM!

WHEN THE SHELLFIRE LIFTED, THE RELIEVING OFFICER YELLED...

C'MON, *EASY!* COME DOWN OUT OF YOUR POSITIONS! ONE BY ONE! SO YOU SHOULDN'T DRAW FIRE! AND WE'LL TAKE OVER ONE BY ONE TOO!

BUT--THE ONLY ANSWER THAT CAME FROM THE MEN OF *EASY...*

HA! HA! HA! HA! HA! HA!

FROM EVERY SHELL-BLASTED HOLE MANNED BY THE BATTERED MEN OF *EASY* ON *SNAKEHEAD HILL*-- CAME THE SAME ANSWER...

HA! HA! HA! HA!

HA! HA! HA!

HA! HA! HA!

AGAIN THE OFFICER YELLED...

WHAT'S THE MATTER WITH YOU MEN? YOU COMBAT-HAPPY? THERE'S AN ATTACK COMING! YOU'RE IN NO CONDITION TO HOLD! YOU'VE DONE YOUR JOB! I ORDER YOU TO LEAVE YOUR LINES ONE BY ONE-- SO WE CAN TAKE OVER!

AGAIN THERE WAS NOTHING BUT LAUGHTER IN RE-TURN--UNTIL EVEN THE ENEMY HEARD IT...

HA! HA! HA!

THE AMERIKANERS ARE OUT OF THEIR HEADS! THEY WILL BE AN EASY VICTORY! THEN WE WILL CRUSH THE RELIEVING COMPANY!

AGAIN THE ENEMY GUNS LAID DOWN A THUNDERING STORM OF FIRE...

THE ATTACK'S STARTING! THEY'VE CUT US OFF FROM *EASY*--BEFORE WE COULD TAKE OVER FROM THEM!

EASY'LL NEVER BE ABLE TO HOLD! WE'LL BE CLOBBERED!

WHAM!

BLAM!

BAM!

THE MEN OF *EASY* WERE STILL LAUGHING AS THEY STOOD LIKE STATUES AT THEIR POSITIONS...

TOO BAD WE COULDN'T TELL OUR RELIEF-- THE *JOKE!*

YEAH-- *SOME* JOKE TOO!

HA! HA! HA! HA!

WHAM!

BAM!

BLAM!

THEN THE SHELLFIRE LIFTED... AND THEY SAW THE ENEMY...

LOOKS LIKE THEY'RE GOIN' TO THROW THE KITCHEN SINK AT US!

AND THE ENEMY SAW THE MEN OF *EASY*...

THEY ARE TOO FROZEN WITH FEAR TO EVEN FIRE! LOOK AT THEM! STANDING LIKE SNOW MEN!

BAM!

THE *ROCK OF EASY CO.* WAS STILL LAUGHING INSIDE OF HIM AS...

WE'LL HAVE TO TAKE OUT THOSE TANKS FIRST! BAZOOKAMEN-- YOU CAN'T TAKE A CHANCE ON A DIRECT HIT! LET THEM COME IN BETWEEN YOU!

CHECK!

THE ENEMY TANKS RUMBLED NEARER AND NEARER TO THE MOTIONLESS MEN OF EASY IN THEIR SHELL-BLASTED HOLES...

RATATATATATATAT!

BEFOW!

BWEE!

ZTING!

49

LIKE SCARECROWS, THE MEN OF **EASY** STOOD AT THEIR POSITIONS AND LET THE TANKS COME IN BETWEEN THEM--BEFORE THEY FIRED...

LOOKS LIKE THESE CHARACTERS NEVER HEARD OF THE SANDWICH PUNCH!

BAM!

BLAAANG!

BUT EVEN THOUGH THEY LOST THEIR ARMOR--THE TOUGH ENEMY TROOPS HURLED THEMSELVES AT THE BATTERED FIGURES OF **EASY**...

THEY HAVE TO COME OUT OF THEIR HOLES NOW--OR WE WILL BE UPON THEM!

RATATATAT! CRACK! CRACK!

BUT THE MEN OF **EASY** LED BY THEIR ROCK-LIKE SERGEANT--STOOD WHERE THEY WERE...

THE ENEMY DOESN'T KNOW THE JOKE EITHER!

POW!

POW!

KPOW!

THE ENEMY LEAPED INTO THE HOLES THE MEN OF **EASY** HAD HELD FOR SO LONG--LIKE A GREAT HUMAN WAVE CRASHING AGAINST A BATTERED WALL...

FOOLS! IF YOU HAD FALLEN BACK--YOU WOULD HAVE SAVED YOUR LIVES!

WE CAN'T, BUSTER! THAT'S THE JOKE!

SEIZING ADVANTAGE OF A LULL IN THE BARRAGE-- THE RELIEVING COMPANY CREPT TOWARDS THE EASY POSITIONS...

THE ENEMY IS PROBABLY MANNING THE *EASY* POSITIONS BY NOW! GET SET FOR A FIRE FIGHT!

BUT, TO THEIR SURPRISE...

YOU STOPPED THEM! *YOU STOPPED THEM!* BUT HOW? *HOW?*

AND THEN WHEN THE OFFICER SAW THE FACES OF *EASY COMPANY*--HE KNEW--SOMEHOW HE KNEW...

THEY'RE OUT ON THEIR FEET! TOO EXHAUSTED TO MOVE-- TO SLEEP--TO EAT-- TO DO ANYTHING-- BUT *MAN* THEIR POSITIONS!

LATER, WHEN ALLIED AIR AND ARTILLERY CRUSHED ENEMY FIRE AND THE MEN OF *EASY* COULD BE MOVED...

THE ONLY THING THAT KEPT THEM GOING -- WAS THEIR FIGHTING HEART!

THAT'S *EASY COMPANY!*

The End

51

THE WAR WAS AS FULL OF THEM AS ANTS AT A SUNDAY PICNIC! BUT THERE WAS ONE THING THEY ALL KNEW — THERE JUST WASN'T ENOUGH ROOM FOR ALL OF THEM!

GUN JOCKEY!

I SUPPOSE YOU THINK YOU'RE LOOKING AT A *P-38* PILOT?

I SUPPOSE YOU THINK THERE'S NO DOUBT ABOUT IT--BECAUSE I'M SIGNING FOR MY SHIP!

OR BECAUSE THIS IS A ONE-MAN "OFFICE" AND I'M THE **ONLY** MAN CLIMBING IN?

OR BECAUSE I'M TAKING THIS SHIP OFF THE GROUND?

NEGATIVE! I'M JUST A **GUN** JOCKEY!

AND MY JOB IS TO BOOT THESE GUNS TO THE FINISH LINE--NO MATTER WHAT GETS IN MY WAY! I'M JUST A JOCKEY FOR SIX FLYING GUNS! AND I'M ONLY ALLOWED TO LOSE **ONCE**--IN THIS RACE!

ONE OTHER THING ABOUT BEING A FLYING *GUN JOCKEY!*

YOU MAY START OUT ALONE IN THIS RACE--

BUT YOU NEVER CAN TELL WHEN *OTHER* JOCKEYS MAY JOIN IN THE RUN!

THE ENEMY PILOTS AREN'T ANY DIFFERENT EITHER--

THEY'RE JUST *GUN JOCKEYS* TOO--

THEY'RE JUST *FLYING GUNS* TO A FINISH LINE TOO!

AND RIGHT NOW--TWO OF THEM HAVE JOINED THIS RACE! AND IF IT'S UP TO THEM--THEY'LL BOX ME IN TO A *FINISH*--UNLESS I CAN GET *OUT* OF THE BOX!

THE GUNS ARE WAITING FOR ME TO JOCKEY THEM INTO POSITION!

THEY'RE WAITING FOR ME TO BOOT THEM WITHIN SIGHT OF THE FINISH LINE TAPE!

BECAUSE IF THEY DON'T SEE IT--IT'LL BE OUR LAST RACE!

CAN'T CLIMB--! IF I DO--I'LL CLIMB RIGHT INTO THE SIGHTS OF THE **GUN JOCKEY UNDER** ME! CAN'T DIVE--! IF I DO--I'LL DIVE RIGHT INTO THE SIGHTS OF THE **GUN JOCKEY OVER** ME!

SO I'LL STAY RIGHT WHERE I AM AS LONG AS POSSIBLE-- RIGHT IN **BETWEEN** THESE TWO **GUN JOCKEYS**!

RATATA

LUFTWAFFE

RATATATATATATATATA

AND I'LL PULL OUT ONLY AT THE VERY LAST MOMENT--AND THAT MOMENT HAS **JUST** ARRIVED!

RATTA-TA-

VROOSH!!

RATTA-TA-

WHILE THOSE *GUN JOCKEYS* ARE USING ALL THEIR FINGERS AND TOES TRYING TO GET OUT OF EACH OTHER'S WAY...

I'LL JOCKEY MY GUNS INTO POSITION ALONG THE FENCE AND SHOW THEM THE FINISH LINE!

THAT'S ONE *GUN JOCKEY* OUT OF THIS RACE! WHERE'S THE OTHER? AS LONG AS HE'S STILL AROUND--I MAY NOT BE AROUND TO FINISH!

THAT OTHER *GUN JOCKEY* IS CHEWING UP ALL MY CONTROLS!

TZING

TZING!

THOUGHT I COULD DIVE AWAY FROM HIM-- BUT HE'S RIDING RIGHT INTO MY COCKPIT!

RA-TA-TA-TA-TAT

MY GUNS ARE NO GOOD--THEY'RE FACING IN THE *WRONG* DIRECTION! THEY'RE WAITING FOR ME TO JOCKEY THEM BACK INTO THE RACE!

I'LL HAVE TO PULL UP NOW--UNLESS I WANT TO START MOWING THAT FIELD! THAT *GUN JOCKEY* ON MY BACK--WILL HAVE TO LOOK OUT FOR HIMSELF-- I'M NOT GOING TO GIVE HIM ANY SIGNALS!

RA-TA-TA-TA-TA

CAN'T SEE MUCH--UNTIL I GET ALL THIS HAY OUT OF MY EYES!

WHOOSH!

LOOKS LIKE THAT *GUN JOCKEY* HAD TO LEAP-FROG RIGHT OVER ME-- TO AVOID LANDING ON A HAYSTACK!

ONE OF THE FIRST RULES ABOUT BEING A *GUN JOCKEY*-- YOU'VE GOT TO LEARN TO KEEP OUT OF THE WAY OF OTHER *GUN JOCKEYS*!

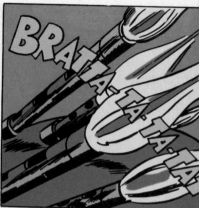

BECAUSE THERE JUST ISN'T *ENOUGH ROOM* IN THE SKIES FOR ALL THE *GUN JOCKEYS* IN THIS WAR!

WHAAM!

ALL THAT MONEY SPENT ON ME --ALL THE TRAINING--!

ALL THAT EQUIPMENT-- AND WHAT FOR?

JUST TO MAKE ME A *GUN JOCKEY*!

58

THEY CALL ME THE CAPTAIN OF A SUBMARINE! BUT WHAT AM I REALLY?

I'M JUST A *GUN JOCKEY!* MAYBE I SHOOT *TNT* FISH INSTEAD OF BULLETS -- BUT I'M STILL A *GUN JOCKEY!*

THE ONLY DIFFERENCE BE- TWEEN ME AND THE OTHER *GUN JOCKEYS* -- IS THAT I USUALLY RUN MY RACE *UNDERWATER!*

BLAANG!

BLAANG!

BUT IF I DON'T JOCKEY MY GUNS INTO FIRING POSITION AGAINST OTHER *GUN JOCKEYS* DROPPING DEPTH CHARGES -- I'LL STAY UNDER- WATER FOR GOOD!

BLAANG!

U S NAVY

THAT ENEMY *GUN JOCKEY* TOPSIDE --

--IS DROPPING THOSE DEPTH CHARGES --

BLAANG!

--RIGHT DOWN OUR CONNING TOWER!

BLAANG!

WHEN YOU CAN'T STAY DOWN--THERE'S ONLY ONE THING TO DO! *TAKE 'ER UP!*

PREPARE TO FIRE!

BLAAANG!

BLAANG!

THERE'S THAT *GUN JOCKEY*-- STILL DROPPING DEPTH CHARGES WHERE WE'RE *NOT!*

7

FIRE ONE! FIRE TWO!

THAT ENEMY *GUN JOCKEY* IS SWIVELING ALL HIS DECK GUNS ON US--TO BLAST US OUT OF THE WATER! WE'LL NEVER BE ABLE TO DIVE OUT OF RANGE FAST ENOUGH! IT'S UP TO THE *TIN FISH* WE'VE JUST SHOT TO TAKE US OFF THIS BULL'S-EYE--BEFORE WE'RE PASTED ON IT--*PERMANENTLY!*

IT'S A RACE NOW BETWEEN THOSE TWO TIN FISH --

AND ALL THE ENEMY'S DECK GUNS --!

BLAM!

THE *GUN JOCKEYS* HAVE DONE THEIR PARTS -- THE REST IS UP TO THE GUNS!

VROOM!

YOU WOULDN'T THINK THAT THERE JUST *ISN'T* ENOUGH ROOM IN ALL THE SEVEN SEAS -- WHEN *GUN JOCKEYS* MEET -- BUT THAT'S THE WAY OF THE WAR!

I'M JUST AN UNDERWATER *GUN JOCKEY* -- THAT'S ALL I REALLY AM --!

WITH GILLS AND...

...FINS...

THEY CALL ME COMBAT INFANTRY! BUT THERE'S ANOTHER NAME FOR ME THAT REALLY FITS *! GUN JOCKEY* ! THAT'S ALL I REALLY AM !

I EAT WITH IT--SLEEP WITH IT ! I'M JUST A PAIR OF HANDS AND..

A PAIR OF FEET CARRYING IT ALONG ON A PACE THAT NEVER ENDS..

I'M JUST A *GUN JOCKEY* WHO KEEPS HIS GUN FROM GETTING WET--EVEN THOUGH I MAY BE DROWNING !

I CLEAN IT--EVEN THOUGH I CAN'T REMEMBER WHEN *I'VE* LAST HAD A BATH !

I FEED IT--EVEN THOUGH I CAN'T REMEMBER WHEN I'VE LAST HAD ANYTHING BUT K-RATIONS !

THERE ARE *GUN JOCKEYS* ON BOTH SIDES OF THIS WAR ! SOME YOU SEE--AND SOME YOU DON'T SEE !

BEE-OWW!

IF YOU CAN'T SEE THE *GUN JOCKEY* THAT SEES YOU--YOU DON'T LAST IN THIS WAR !

IF THE ONLY WAY I CAN JOCKEY MY GUN CLOSER TO THAT ENEMY *GUN JOCKEY*--IS BY GIVING HIM A CLOSER BEAD ON MY HELMET--GUESS THAT'S HOW IT'LL HAVE TO BE!

THAT'S CLOSE ENOUGH!

SPAANG!

THIS IS CLOSER!

KPOW!

KPOW!

HIDDEN PILLBOX--! THAT'S WHAT THAT TREETOP *GUN JOCKEY* WAS PROTECTING!

TAKKA-TAKKA!

BEEOW!

ZING!

IF I JOCKEY MY GUN INTO THE RIGHT POSITION--IT DOESN'T NEED MUCH ROOM TO OPER-ATE! ALMOST ANYTHING'LL DO! A VIEW SLIT, FOR IN-STANCE--IF THERE'S AMMO BEHIND IT!

BLAM!

POW! POW!

A *GUN JOCKEY* LIKE ME--NEVER SEES MUCH OF THE WAR HE'S FIGHTING IN! THINK I'LL CLIMB UP ON THAT GUN--THAT SOME OTHER GUN JOCKEY LEFT--AND TAKE A LOOK AROUND!

EVERYBODY'S A *GUN JOCKEY!* I'M A WALKING ONE--AND THAT BUZZARD'S A FLYING ONE! BUT IT'S ALL THE SAME IN THE END--

TAKKA - TAKKA!

BANG! BWEE! BROW!

THERE'S NEVER ENOUGH ROOM FOR ALL THE *GUN JOCKEYS* AROUND--*WALKING--SWIMMING--RIDING--FLYING* ONES! THERE'S NEVER ENOUGH ROOM!

POW! POW! POW!

LOOK AT HIM, GENTLEMEN! A REAL FIGHTING MAN! YOU CAN'T TELL THE DIFFERENCE BETWEEN HIM AND HIS GUN!

HE IS THE GUN!

The End

THAT ENEMY TANK ON TOP OF *NO-RETURN HILL*--WAS IT ABOUT TO RAIN DOWN STEEL ON TOP OF OUR 'TIN POTS¿ OR WAS IT AS SILENT AS THE SMOKE RISIN' UP FROM IT¿ IT WAS A RIDDLE ONLY *FOUR GUYS FROM EASY COMPANY* COULD SOLVE FOR US! AND NONE OF 'EM COULD TALK-- NO MATTER HOW MUCH WE YELLED:

CALLING EASY CO..!

THEY CALL ME *"THE ROCK OF EASY COMPANY"*...I'M SUPPOSED TO BE TOUGHER THAN TOUGH!

BUT, I'LL TELL YOU SOME-THIN' I'D NEVER LET *EASY* KNOW! SOMETIMES, THE THINGS THESE CHARACTERS DO-- *SPLIT ME WIDE OPEN!*

LIKE WHAT HAPPENED THAT NIGHT ON *NO-RETURN HILL!*

"It started when I gave the sign to four jokers of Easy..."

INTELLIGENCE SAYS *NO-RETURN HILL* IS CLEAR - FOR THE MOMENT- AFTER THE DUSTIN' *AIR* GAVE IT! YOU GUYS'LL HAVE TO HOLD IT-- UNTIL I CAN GET THE REST OF THE COMPANY TOGETHER TO REINFORCE YOU! THAT'LL TAKE TILL MORNIN'!

IF YOU *DON'T* HOLD IT-- THE ENEMY'LL BE *UP* THERE-LOOKIN' *DOWN* OUR THROATS WHEN WE ATTACK THE HILL TOMORROW MORNIN'!

"Whenever things were toughest, you could always count on the jokers of Easy to kid the most..."

WE'LL EXPECT AT LEAST AN *EXTRA* CAN OF K-RATIONS FOR THIS JOB, SGT ROCK!

YEAH -- NONE OF THIS TIN HARDWARE STUFF-I'M ALLERGIC TO MEDALS, SARGE!

"It took me most of the night to collect Easy... scattered after a couple o' days o' rugged fightin'... then we started for No-Return Hill..."

WONDER WHAT WE'LL FIND WHEN WE GET THERE?

"We weren't fired on as we started up No-Return Hill -- but that didn't mean a thing..."

THE FOUR GUYS I LEFT HERE WOULDN'T FIRE...

AND THE *ENEMY* WOULDN'T! UNTIL WE WERE SO FAR UP THE HILL -- WE COULDN'T SCRAMBLE *BACK* IN TIME-ONCE THEY OPENED UP!

"When you've top-kicked an outfit as long as I have -- you know exactly what they're thinkin'..."

THEY'RE THINKIN' THE *SAME THING!* BUT- NOT ONE OF 'EM IS MISSIN' A SINGLE STEP -- BECAUSE THEY'RE *EASY COMPANY!*

"And then I saw him... lyin' like a figure of stone on a heap of stone rocks ... "

"It was one of the four men I had sent out to hold the hill... and from the signs o' fightin' all around him..."

HE HELD HIS GROUND AS LONG AS HE COULD -- THEN THE ENEMY MOVED UP WITH A *TANK!* AN' WE DON'T HAVE A *BAZOOKA!* WONDER WHAT HAPPENED? WONDER WHO'S AHEAD OF US? THE *ENEMY?* OR *OUR GUYS?*

"The men tried to take his rifle out of his hands -- "

SARGE -- WE CAN'T MAKE HIM LET GO!

HE WOULDN'T LET *ANYONE* TAKE IT FROM HIM! THAT'S A REAL *EASY MAN!* LET HIM KEEP IT!

"As the first aid men moved down with him— I knew what was on everyone's mind as we moved up..."

THEY'RE WONDERIN' WHAT'S AHEAD OF 'EM! THEY'RE WONDERIN' WHAT HAPPENED HERE YESTERDAY WHEN THE FOUR GUYS WERE HOLDIN' THE HILL!

"It wasn't until later that we learned... about the four men..."

"No-Return Hill sent chills down their backs even though it was clear... just as Intelligence had reported..."

WE'VE GOT A BREAK FOR ONCE! THE ENEMY'S NOT UP THERE --IN FRONT OF US -- WAITIN' FOR US!

IF THEY'RE NOT UP THERE -- THAT MEANS THEY'RE BEHIND US! SOME FUN!

"Easy guys have been fightin' so long that they 'write the book' as they go along ...and after they had gone up about a quarter of the way..."

I CAN'T STAND HEIGHTS! MAKES ME DIZZY! I'LL DIG IN HERE!

"The other three guys didn't say anythin'...but bein' from Easy...all were thinkin' the same thing..."

SID'S PICKIN' THE TOUGHEST POSITION FOR HIMSELF!

HE'S GOIN' TO HAVE TO MEET THE ENEMY FIRST!

"Sid shoved a little cover in front of him—and waited..."

WONDER HOW LONG BEFORE THEY PUT IN A BID FOR THIS CHUNK OF REAL ESTATE -- WITH TNT BIDS?

"If you'd have asked Sid how long he waited..."

"You'd need a different kind of watch than civilians use..."

"One that measures a year of waitin' for every second..."

"Then, a white-hot sun exploded in front of Sid's eyes..."

BAM

POTATO MASHER--! DIDN'T HEAR 'EM SNEAK UP!

"Half-blinded by the glare, he really couldn't see the next Potato Masher that sailed in out of the dark--but he heard it land!"

IT'S-- RIGHT HERE!

THUD

"He fumbled for it..."

IT'S RIGHT HERE-- RIGHT HERE-- WHERE IS IT?

"His fingers clawed for that stick of TNT-- knowin' every second that ticked by-- was a second less he had to live..."

WHERE IS IT-- WHERE IS IT?

"Only his heart beats could tell you how long it took for him to find the Potato Masher and flip it away..."

HOW MUCH TIME LEFT BEFORE IT GOES OFF--? HOW MUCH TIME?

"The explodin' Potato Masher answered him-- he just made it!"

THEY'RE RIGHT ON THE HEELS OF THEIR OWN FIRE-WORKS!

WHAM

"Sid settled himself for the rest of the enemy attack..."

I'VE GOTTA SOFTEN UP--

"As if he had a 99-year lease on the position..."

--THOSE BUZZARDS--

"But he was an Easy Man-- so he wasn't foolin' himself!"

--FOR THE OTHER GUYS!

POW

KPOW

POW

KPOW

KPOW

KPOW

"He fired until he saw it comin'..."

TANK! GUESS THEY KNOW EASY'S HOLDIN' THIS HILL AND IT'LL TAKE MORE THAN INFANTRY TO KICK US OFF!

KLANK KLANK

"The Tank came on-- like it knew Sid had nothin' to stop it with - except his heart!"

RATATATAT

"Sid had nothin' left to fight the enemy tank with..."

POW

GOT TO CONCENTRATE ON THE SLITS--

"Except the heart of an *Easy Man*... and rifle clips..."

KPOW

MAYBE THE RICOCHETS'LL--

"And he fought as long as he was able..."

SOFTEN 'EM UP INSIDE!

KPOW

POW

POW KPOW

POW KPOW

KLICK

KLICK

"Sid never left his post... it's a rule of Easy's -- you won't find it written down - but -- no one's broken it!!"

KLANK KLANK

"If he could have talked... that was the story he would have told us, as we looked back at him as he was taken down No-Return Hill..."

HE DID WHAT HE HAD TO DO! NOW--*WE* HAVE TO DO WHAT *WE* HAVE TO DO!

"We slogged on up the hill... drippin' icy sweat..."

WHAT HAPPENED TO THE OTHER THREE GUYS--WHEN THE TANK AND INFANTRY MOVED UP? *WHO'S* WAITIN' FOR US UP THERE? *THEM*--OR *OUR GUYS*? *THEM*?... OR...?

"We followed the tracks of the tank and the infantry until we saw two other Easy guys..."

SARGE! IT'S MACK AND AL! LOOK AT 'EM! SITTIN' BACK TO BACK! EVER SEE ANYTHIN' LIKE THIS, SARGE?

YOU GET TO SEE EVERY-THIN' IN EASY-- SOONER OR LATER!

"As I watched the first aid men take Mack and Al down the hill..."

THEY'RE WONDERIN' WHAT HAPPENED HERE? WHY TWO MEN STAYED? WHY THEY FOUGHT BACK TO BACK!

"Mack was never a guy for words... he probably would've grunted if you'd asked him..."

"But his pal, Al, liked to talk more than almost anythin'-- and he would've told us what had happened after Sid had been left on the lower part of No-Return Hill..."

I'LL SET UP HOUSE-KEEPIN' HERE! I'LL HAVE NOTHIN' TO DO! SID'LL PIN BACK THEIR EARS ANY-WAY!

"The last two men of the patrol glanced at the terrain... bare of cover like the out-side of a ping-pong ball... and knew that Al had cut himself a hard piece of cake... that was when Mack dropped out with a grunt..."

"The ground was too hard for the men to dig in-- so they just lay down-- facin' downhill..."

IF I WANTED COMPANY-- AT LEAST I MIGHT HAVE DRAWN SOMEONE WHO WASN'T A BLUEPRINT FOR A SPHINX!

"An' Mack answered in the only vocabulary he ever used-- with a grunt..."

"They both heard the firin' from Sid's position down the hill... and saw the darkness lit up by the flashes of potato Mashers..."

LOOKS LIKE SID IS GIVIN' THEM A REAL PARTY! I TOLD YOU WE'D HAVE NOTHIN' TO DO!

RATATATAT

KPOW-KPOW POW

POW

"Then the sounds of firin' stopped... and there was nothin' but blackness all around us..."

THAT WAS A TANK DOWN THERE, MACK! THINK MAYBE SID GOT IT! IT'S POSSIBLE TO BLOW OFF ITS TREADS WITH GRENADES-- SLOW IT UP-- FIRE THROUGH THE SLITS AND--

"Al stopped..."

"Because the darkness answered him..."

"And the answer was loud and clear..."

KLANK-KLANKETY-KLANK-KLANK

73

"Like I said: Easy Guys always wrote the book as they went along -- Mack just grunted as he gathered up all their grenades -- but Al knew what he was goin' to do..."

GO ON, MACK! YOU'RE COVERED! DO YOUR PLANTIN'!

"And Mack 'planted' seeds of TNT from where the tank was comin' through the dark..."

KLANKETY-KLANK KLANK

"Right up towards their position..."

NEATEST JOB OF "PLANTIN'" I EVER SAW! BET YOU WERE A FARMER IN CIVVIE LIFE, HUH, MACK?

"Mack answered with the grunt that was his way of speakin'... then he an' Al waited..."

BLANG

THERE'S THE FIRST SEED SPROUTIN'! RIGHT UNDER THAT CAN!

"After the next two explosions..."

BAM BLAM

THE TANK'S STOPPED! WE DID IT, MACK! WE DID IT!

"But Mack answered him with a grunt... and Al understood... as the rest of the grenades went off!"

WHAM BAM BLAM

THE TANK'S STOPPED -- TO LET INFANTRY OUTFLANK US!

"So Al and Mack fought back to back so they could cover both flanks..."

SAY, MACK! WHAT DO YOU DO WHEN YOU PHONE ANYBODY? GRUNT TWICE FOR YES? AND ONCE FOR NO?

BRATATAT

POW
KPOW
KPOW

KLICK
KLICK

"Al never got his answer... because Mack only grunted as he fired until he ran dry..."

CLICK
CLICK

"Those two were the best shots in the outfit...they stopped the enemy infantry with their last bullets...then the tank opened up..."

RATATAT

KLANK
KLANK
KLANK

"Like Sid--Al and Mack followed Easy's unwritten rule--they never left their position...as the tank went on..."

"Yeah--we never could've found out from Mack what happened... but Nick would've told us..."

THE TANK'S STILL AHEAD OF US! ALL THE SIGNS POINT TO IT GOIN' ON! THERE'S NOTHIN' TO STOP IT NOW -- BUT NICK!

"We went on... and everyone knew what everyone else was thinkin'..."

NICK JUST JOINED THE OUTFIT! WE HAD TO USE HIM--BECAUSE THERE WAS NO ONE LEFT! WE DON'T KNOW IF HE'LL HOLD UP! WE DON'T KNOW IF HE'S REALLY AN EASY MAN!

75

"The silence grew and grew..."

WHO'S WAITIN' FOR US UP THERE?

"Until it knotted around our throats..."

NICK--?

"Like a noose..."

OR THE TANK?

"As we got to the top, everyone saw the tank lookin' down at us... and I didn't have to yell FLATTEN!"

IT'S GOT US RIGHT IN ITS SIGHTS!-- AND US WITHOUT A BAZOOKA!

NICK COULDN'T HOLD IT!--CAN'T BLAME THE KID! HE HADN'T BEEN IN EASY LONG ENOUGH FOR EASY'S COMBAT HEART TO RUB OFF ON HIM!

"Suddenly I realized..."

THE TANK'S NOT FIRIN' AT US! IT'S SMOKIN'!

"I motioned the guys down... and snaked up to the tank... and then... when the smoke parted... I saw him!"

IT'S NICK!-- LYIN' ON TOP!

76

"As I hustled to the top of the tank, I read all the signs..."

WITHOUT INFANTRY-- THE TANK HAD LOST ITS "EYES"!

ANYBODY WHO DIDN'T KNOW-- WOULD'VE SAID THE TANK WAS SLOWED UP-- THAT NICK SNEAKED UP ON IT-- AND FIRED INTO THE VIEWSLIT-- UNTIL SOMETHIN' INSIDE BLEW!

BUT US GUYS OF EASY KNOW IT WAS THE KID'S FIGHTIN' HEART THAT BROKE DOWN STEEL! THAT HE WAS AN EASY MAN-- BEFORE HE EVEN JOINED EASY!

YEAH-- THAT'S THE WAY IT IS IN EASY COMPANY-- WHERE NOTHIN' IS EASY!

The End

I'M SGT. ROCK OF EASY CO... AND LOTS OF TIMES IT AIN'T **EASY** TO BE A **SERGEANT**--AND IT SURE AIN'T EASY BEIN' IN **EASY COMPANY**!

ESPECIALLY WHEN YOU HAVE TO LEAD MEN ACROSS AN OPEN FIELD...

THE GUYS ARE THINKIN' OUT SO LOUD--I CAN HEAR 'EM!

CROSSIN' THAT'LL MAKE FLIES UNDER A FLY SWATTER OUT'VE US!

I'LL BET ENEMY ARTILLERY IS WATCHIN' US RIGHT AT THIS VERY MINUTE!

I CAN FEEL A MILLION SIGHTS PASTED RIGHT ONTO MY TIN POT!

THE LONGER YOU WAIT--THE WORSE IT GETS-- SO I STARTED 'EM GOIN'!

KEEP A SKIRMISH LINE! START SLOW--SO YOU'LL HAVE PLENTY OF WIND LEFT--IN CASE YOU HAVE TO START GALLOPIN'! LET'S GO!

I KEPT MY EYE ON THE KID... HE HADN'T BEEN IN ACTION YET... BUT HE WAS SWEATIN' AWAY TO A SHADOW...

NOT TOO CLOSE, KID! THERE'S MORE SAFETY IN BEIN' ALONE--WHEN YOU CROSS AN OPEN FIELD!

S-S-SURE, SARGE-- I--I F-FORGOT--!

IT WAS SO QUIET CROSSIN'...

I COULD HEAR EVERY HEART BEATIN'...

AS IF IT WOULD RIP RIGHT THROUGH THE CLOTH ...

THERE WAS A RIPPIN' SOUND ALL RIGHT--BUT IT WAS THE AIR BEIN' RIPPED--AND THEN THE GROUND!

OKAY, *EASY!* FROM NOW ON--ROLL OUT ALL THE STOPS UNTIL WE REACH THE WOODS!

VOOMP!

WHAM!

THE WOODS MEANT COVER--BUT THE SHELLS SLAMMIN' DOWN--MOVED THE WOODS FURTHER BACK THAN THE MOON!

SHELLIN' IS LIKE SUBTRACTION... *YOU* CAN BE IN THE MIDDLE RUNNIN' WITH TWO OTHER GUYS... LIKE THE KID...

AND FIND YOURSELF ALONE -- THAT'S WHAT HAPPENED TO THE KID...

BLAM!

WHEN TWO OTHER GUYS MOVED UP TO FILL THE GAP... THE KID WAS NOW ON THE END...'

BUT THE SUBTRACTION WENT ON...

BLAM!

WHEN WE FINALLY GOT TO THE WOODS I REMEMBERED I WAS THE SERGEANT -- AND THAT THINGS ARE NEVER EASY IN *EASY CO.* ...

KEEP GOIN'! *KEEP GOIN'!* YOU KNOW THEY'LL SHELL THE EDGE OF THE WOODS!

WE AIN'T A *ROCK-- LIKE--YOU-- SARGE..!*

THEY STUMBLED AND DRAGGED THEMSELVES AWAY FROM THE DANGER OF LIFTIN' FIRE -- BUT WHEN I LOOKED AT THEM ...

THEY'VE *HAD* IT-- ESPECIALLY THE *KID!* UNLESS I KIN MAKE 'EM *FORGET* WHAT THEY'VE JUST BEEN THROUGH!

I DIDN'T LET 'EM KNOW THAT THE MATCH I TRIED TO STRIKE-SEEMED TO WEIGH A TON...

THAT I REALLY HAD NO BREATH LEFT TO PUFF THE CIGARETTE LIT...

THAT I WAS ACTIN' I *WASN'T* AS BEAT AS THEY WAS !

SWKKK!

I DIDN'T EVEN RECOGNIZE THE CROAK AS MY OWN VOICE ...

SO YOU BUTTERBALLS THINK *THIS* WAS TOUGH ! THERE ARE TOUGHER THINGS THAN DUCKIN' AN ENEMY BARRAGE ! MUCH TOUGHER ! FIGURE 'EM OUT FOR YOURSELVES --IF YOUR BRAINS AIN'T TOO SCRAMBLED !

THEY BEGAN TO PERK UP...BUT IT WAS THE KID I REALLY WAS WATCHIN'!...HE WAS THE MOST FAR GONE...

GUESS...BEIN' HUNG UP IN WIRE...IS TOUGHER...!

OR LETTIN' A TANK ROLL-- OVER YOUR *TIN POT*--WHILE YOU'RE CROUCHED IN A FOXHOLE--!

NO-- THERE ARE *WORSE* THINGS ! MUCH WORSE !

YEAH--IT WAS THE KID I WAS WATCHIN'...BECAUSE IF HE STILL KEPT ON LOOKIN' LIKE A RAG DOLL...HE WOULD HAVE HAD IT...THE FIRST GUY IN *EASY*...AND WE DIDN'T WANT "FIRSTS" LIKE THAT...

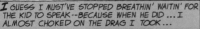

I GUESS I MUST'VE STOPPED BREATHIN' WAITIN' FOR THE KID TO SPEAK--BECAUSE WHEN HE DID...I ALMOST CHOKED ON THE DRAG I TOOK...

WH-WHAT'S...WORSE... THAN...THAT RUN THROUGH...FIRE... SGT. ROCK?

I TOLD HIM THE TRUTH...AND HE WAS HOOKED...

BEIN' FORCED TO LEAVE A MAN BEHIND WHEN YOU'RE IN COMBAT, KID--THAT'S THE HARD WAY!

I COULD SEE THE SHELL-SHOCKED LOOK LEAVIN' THEIR EYES SLOWLY... AS THEY LISTENED...

DID YOU EVER HAVE TO LEAVE A MAN BE-HIND, SARGE?

YEAH, KID! AND I'LL NEVER FOR-GET IT! IT WAS RIGHT AFTER THE INVASION!

"WE WERE PUSHIN' INLAND...OUR ORDERS WERE TO ATTACK A FARMHOUSE COM-MANDIN' A STONE BRIDGE THAT TANKS COULD USE..."

WE STOP FOR NOTHIN' AND NO ONE UNTIL WE SET UP HOUSE-KEEPIN' IN THAT FARMHOUSE! THAT'S THE ORDERS! SO IF ANYONE WANTS TO TURN BACK--NOW'S THE TIME!

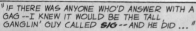

"IF THERE WAS ANYONE WHO'D ANSWER WITH A GAG--I KNEW IT WOULD BE THE TALL, GANGLIN' GUY CALLED SIG--AND HE DID..."

AND MISS A CHANCE FOR A NICE WALK IN THE SUN, SARGE--AFTER ALL THAT TIME WE SPENT COOPED UP ON THE DIRTY GREY OCEAN? NIX!

"SO WE STARTED OUT...AND BECAUSE SIG HAD RUBBER LEGS THAT NEVER TIRED--I SENT HIM OUT AHEAD...AS POINT..."

HE'S SEEN SOMETHIN'! HE WANTS US TO STOP!

"AS I HAD THE MEN WAIT, AND RAN TOWARD SIG-- I SAW HIM BOUNCE AROUND ON THE ROAD..."

HE'S BEEN HIT BY MACHINE GUN FIRE!

VIIP! ZIIP! VIIP!

"I WAS TOO FAR AWAY TO HELP HIM... BUT I COULD SEE SIG ROLL OUT OF THE WAY OF A HEAVILY-ARMED *NAZI RECON CAR*..."

RATATAT!

"THAT *RECON CAR* WAS HEADIN' STRAIGHT FOR US... AND IT HAD PLENTY OF LEAD TO WASTE..."

RATAT!

"BUT IT FORGOT A GUY FROM *EASY* BY THE NAME OF SIG... WHO NEVER STOPPED PITCHIN'!"

HERE'S YOUR TRANSFER!

PLING!

"SIG'S 'TRANSFER' WAS STAMPED WITH *T.N.T.*... AND IT KNOCKED THE *RECON CAR* OFF THE TRACKS!"

WHAAM!

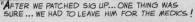

"WE WERE WITHIN SIGHT OF THE FARMHOUSE WHEN WE HEARD SMALL ARMS FIRE BEHIND US...!"

SARGE--THAT'S SIG'S THOMPSON!

I GOT EARS!

BUDDA! BUDDA!

"THE THOMPSON RATTLED AWAY UNTIL IT WAS EMPTY-- THEN--WE HEARD ENEMY BURP GUN FIRE...!"

BRRR!

BRRRP!

"THEN--WE HEARD THE SOUND OF GRENADES BEIN' TOSSED ONE AFTER THE OTHER...!"

WHIAM!

BLAM!

"THEN--WE HEARD NOTHIN'-- JUST NOTHIN'!--AND IT WAS THE LONELIEST SOUND IN THE WORLD..."

"ANYBODY CAN CARRY OUT EASY ORDERS...IT TAKES A SERGEANT TO CARRY OUT THE RUGGED ONES...I WAS A REAL SERGEANT--I HAD TO PROVE IT...NOW!"

THE WAR'S THAT WAY!

"THE FARMHOUSE WAS FILLED WITH THE ENEMY-- THEY OPENED UP ON US AS WE GOT NEAR THE STONE FENCE..."

WE CAN PLAY IT SAFE AND STAY BEHIND THAT STONE FENCE-- OR TAKE THIS PLACE FOR SIG!

LET'S TAKE IT FOR SIG!

VIIP! VIIP! VIIP! VIIP!

"WE WEREN'T FIGHTIN' BY THE BOOK--WE WERE FIGHTIN' FOR SIG--AND WE DID THINGS THE ENEMY DIDN'T EXPECT!"

THIS IS FOR SIG!

BUDDA!

"A GUY WOULD TOSS A PINEAPPLE EVEN AFTER HE WAS KO'D..."

FOR...

RATAT!

VHP!

VHP! VHP!

--SIG!

WHAM!

"WELL, WE GOT THE FARMHOUSE, AND WATCHED OUR TANKS GO OVER THE BRIDGE TO BLAST THE WAY FOR INFANTRY..."

A LOT OF DOGTAGS WON'T BE COLLECTED BECAUSE OF THOSE TANKS -- AND SIG...

YEAH--!

CLANK! CLANK!

I KNEW WHAT THE KID WAS GOIN' TO ASK THE MOMENT I FINISHED TELLIN' THE STORY...

WHAT ABOUT SIG, SARGE? WHAT HAPPENED TO HIM?

SADDLE UP, MEN! WE'VE GOT A CROSSROADS TO TAKE! AND WE CAN'T STOP FOR NO ONE -- OR NOTHIN'! LET'S GO!

THE KID KEPT ON ASKIN'--UNTIL I HAD TO TELL HIM...

I DON'T KNOW WHAT HAPPENED TO SIG, KID! IT'S ONE OF THOSE THINGS ABOUT FIGHTIN'! YOU LEAVE A MAN BEHIND--AND YOU CAN ONLY GUESS WHAT HAPPENED! YOU DON'T KNOW!

THE *MESSERSCHMITT* PROBABLY ONLY HAD ONE BELT LEFT IN HIS GUNS AS HE WAS RETURN-IN' TO HIS FIELD--AND HE DIDN'T SEE ANY SENSE IN WASTIN' IT!

SCRATCH, CHICKENS!

RAT-AT!

HE WAS GONE! LIKE A SHADOW--BUT HE LEFT A SOUVENIR OF HIS VISIT...

HOW BAD YOU HIT, KID?

THE KID'S ANSWER WOULD'VE BROKEN MY HEART--IF IT WASN'T MADE OF *ROCK*...

WHO'S HIT, SARGE? I JUST *TRIPPED* OVER MY SHOE-LACES!

FOR THE SECOND TIME IN MY LIFE I HAD TO PROVE I WAS A SERGEANT--I DON'T KNOW IF I COULD'VE DONE IT--IF THE KID HADN'T PROVED HE WAS A REAL *EASY* GUY...

HEY, SARGE! I'LL BET I GET A NICE TAN HERE--WHILE YOU'RE STILL LOOKIN' FOR THAT CROSS-ROADS!

YEAH--THEY DON'T CALL ME *ROCK* FOR NOTHIN'...

SEE YOU AFTER THE WAR!

WE LOOKED BACK AT HIM UNTIL WE COULDN'T SEE HIM...AND THEN WE LISTENED AS LONG AS WE COULD HEAR ANYTHIN'... BUT IT WAS DIFFERENT THIS TIME--WORSE EVEN...

NOTHIN'--JUST *NOTHIN'!*

THE CROSSROADS WAS FIXED UP REAL CUTE FOR US... IT WAS GUARDED BY A SUNKEN TANK--THE WORST KIND OF PILLBOX!

FLATTEN!

WHAM!

BAM!

ONCE AGAIN--WE WEREN'T FIGHTIN' BY THE BOOK...

LET'S TAKE IT FOR THE KID!

ZIIP!

ZIIP!

WHAM!

FIGHTIN' A TANK THAT'S BEEN TURNED INTO A PILLBOX--IS LIKE TACKLIN' A SUB WITH A FLY SWATTER BUT...

KEEP GOIN' FOR THE KID!

BUDDA!

RATATAT!

WHAM!

BAM!

OUR BULLETS AND GRENADES BOUNCED OFF THE SUNKEN TANK TURRET LIKE BUTTER BALLS ON A HOT PAN...

ZIIP!

VIIP!

BAM!

VIIP!

RATATAT!

BWEE!

BWEE!

BWEE!

ZIIP!

BUT ENOUGH OF US MANAGED TO GET CLOSE ENOUGH TO POUR ALL THE FIRE WE HAD INTO THE VIEW SLITS UNTIL...

FOR THE KID!

BLANG!

BUDDA!

WE HAD THE CROSSROADS ALL RIGHT-- BUT ANYONE COULD'VE KNOCKED US OVER WITH A PAPER FAN--AND THAT WAS WHEN...

RATATAT!

TANK! WE'VE HAD IT!

THERE WAS NO EXIT FOR EASY THIS TIME -- WE FACED THAT TANK WITH EMPTY GUNS AND WOUNDED MEN...

AND THEN, FOR THE FIRST TIME, WE SAW WHAT HAPPENED TO ONE MAN THAT WAS LEFT BEHIND...

IT'S THE KID! TRYIN' TO GET TO THE VIEW SLITS!

RAT-AT!

RAT-AT!

DON'T ASK ME HOW A GUY LEFT BEHIND FOR THE MEDICS -- OR WORSE -- CAN HAUL HIMSELF UP A TANK AS IT PASSES HIM-- AND CLAW HIS WAY UP HOT STEEL...

BUDDA!

THAT TANK ROLLED RIGHT UP TO US BEFORE THE KID'S SLUGS FINALLY LANDED A KAYO PUNCH IN THE TANK'S AMMO!

BLAM!

DON'T TELL ME THAT THESE THINGS AIN'T IN THE BOOK!

I THOUGHT I'D LET YOU KNOW HOW I WAS MAKIN' OUT AFTER YOU LEFT ME, SARGE!

YEAH -- I KNOW! THIS AIN'T ACCORDIN' TO THE BOOK! BUT-- THAT'S EASY COMPANY FOR YOU!

The END.

⑬

THE "BIG QUESTION" STILL HADN'T BEEN ANSWERED AS WE BOILED INTO THE ENEMY HARBOR IN OUR PICKUP BOAT...

I TELL YOU, TOM--THERE'S NOTHING WORSE THAN MEETING A SHARK!

SHARKS WON'T ATTACK UNLESS YOU BOTHER THEM FIRST!

I'D RATHER FACE T.N.T. THAN ONE OF THOSE SILENT KILLERS!

YES--THE "BIG QUESTION" WAS ONE I'D HAVE TO FIND THE ANSWER TO MYSELF... I'LL FIND OUT ALL ABOUT IT ON THIS JOB! THEY SAY THE WATERS AROUND HERE ARE FILLED WITH SHARKS!

I LOOKED TOWARDS THE SOUTH SIDE OF THE ENEMY-HELD ISLAND,...

THAT'S THE SIDE THAT'S TOO STEEP FOR OUR TROOPS TO HIT!

U.S.N.

BUT THE ENEMY HAD PLACED A SHORE BATTERY IN A CAVE DUG OUT OF THE FACE OF THE CLIFF...

BLAM

AND IT WAS LAYING DOWN MURDEROUS FIRE ON OUR LANDING CRAFT BEFORE THEY EVEN REACHED THE POINT OF DEPARTURE...

WE'VE GOT TO GET THAT GUN! IF WE CAN ONLY GET IN A LITTLE CLOSER BEFORE DROPPING OFF...

PT-213

JUST THEN, LEAD HAIL RATTLED AGAINST THE SIDES OF OUR *PICKUP* BOAT AS..

TAKE OFF-- TAKE OFF!

HEY, TOM!--IF YOU SEE ANY SHARKS-- MAKE BELIEVE YOU'RE A SARDINE-- AND *MAYBE* THEY'LL GO AWAY!

TAKKA TAKKA!

IT WAS THE RAGGEDEST DIVE I HAD EVER MADE--BUT I GOT OUT OF THE RAIN OF SLUGS...

THEY'RE DRAWING THE FIRE AWAY FROM US! MAYBE THE ENEMY DIDN'T SEE US DROP OFF!

THE GRIN I HAD ON MY FACE AT MY BUDDY'S REMARK SUDDENLY FROZE AS I DOVE PAST A BULLET-LIKE FORM ...

SHARK--!

I FLIPPERED AWAY...

HE'S FOLLOWING ME!

I STOPPED...

HE'S STOPPED TOO!

I STARTED AGAIN...

HE'S TAILING ME AGAIN!

As I REACHED THE BOTTOM OF THE CLIFF ON WHICH THE ENEMY BATTERY WAS BASED...

WHEN IS HE GOING TO CHARGE?

BUT THE SHARK WAS A SILENT SHADOW... A WAITING SHADOW...

WHEN--? WHEN--?

I DIDN'T BREATHE ALL THE TIME I KEPT CLAWING FOR HANDHOLDS...UNTIL...

BAM!

I'M OUT OF THE WATER-- I'M OUT OF THE WATER! I GOT AWAY FROM HIM!

BUT I WAS COMING WITHIN RANGE OF THE ENEMY...

TAKKATAKKA!

THEY'VE SPOTTED ME--!

IF THE FACE OF THE CLIFF HADN'T BEEN UNEVEN--I WOULD HAVE BEEN NAILED IMMEDIATELY...

IT'S A TOSSUP--WHETHER I CAN GET WITHIN RANGE TO TOSS A STICK OF T.N.T. AT THEM--BEFORE I LOSE WHATEVER COVER I HAVE-- AND THEY TOSS ME OFF!

TAKKA!

BLAM!

I FINALLY REACHED THE SPOT WHERE I HAD TO MAKE MY PLAY...

HOPE THIS HITS THE MARK--!

ZING

BEEOW

ONLY ONE THING HIT THE MARK--THE BURST WITH WHICH THE ENEMY SWATTED AWAY THE *T.N.T.* STICK...

TAKKA!

I PRIMED ANOTHER STICK...

THIS HAS GOT TO BE IT--!

BEEOW

THIS TIME I DIDN'T EVEN GET TO THROW IT...

THEY'VE LOWERED A GUY TO SWAT ME OFF THE CLIFF--!

THUD!

CAN'T FIGHT HIM--!

--AND TOSS THIS TOO--!

--SO I'LL JUST DUCK-- AND TOSS--!

THE *T.N.T.* STICK LANDED A MOMENT *AFTER* I DOVE OFF THE CLIFF...

WHAAM!

AS I SANK INTO THE WATER LIKE A STONE...

NEVER THOUGHT I'D MAKE IT--! IT'S CLEAR FLIPPERING FROM NOW ON!

THAT'S WHAT I THOUGHT..

THE SHARK'S-- STILL SHADOWING ME!

I WENT ON... HE'S STILL WITH ME!

I STOPPED... HE'S STOPPED TOO!

I KICKED ON AGAIN... WHAT'S HE WAITING FOR--?

IT SEEMED AS IF THERE WAS NOTHING IN THE SEA... NOTHING EXCEPT ME... AND MY SILENT SHADOW...

AND THEN I SAW IT... ANOTHER SHARK—LIKE FORM...

ENEMY SUB-- COMING OUT OF AN UNDERSEA SUB PEN --TO HIT OUR SHIPS!

I HEADED TOWARDS IT... FIGURING I'D BOARD IT... AND PLASTER SOME T.N.T. ONTO IT-- WHEN IT SUDDENLY TURNED SHARPLY-- RAMMING ME WITH THE CONNING TOWER..

THUNGG!

BUT I HADN'T FIGURED ON THE BLOODHOUND TENACITY OF THE GUYS WHO WERE TRACKING DOWN THE ENEMY SUB...

WHOOSH!

WHOOSH!

THEY'RE ON TOP OF US AGAIN--!

THE NEXT MOMENT THE WATER BOILED WITH THE FORCE OF THE EXPLOSION...

WHUMP

DROPPED-- THE T.N.T.--!

AS I FLIPPERED FOR THE T.N.T., I HEARD THE VIBRATIONS OF SCREWS CHURNING BY OVER-HEAD...

THEY'RE PASSING! THEY ALMOST GOT THE SUB! IT'S STILL UP TO ME!

AND THEN-- I FROZE...

THE SHARK'S AT THE T.N.T.!

THERE WAS ONLY ONE THING LEFT TO DO...

GOT TO GET THAT *T.N.T.*--

--BEFORE THE SUB--

--GETS AWAY FROM ME!

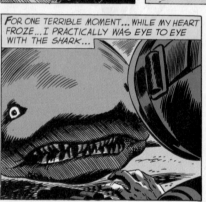

FOR ONE TERRIBLE MOMENT...WHILE MY HEART FROZE...I PRACTICALLY WAS EYE TO EYE WITH THE SHARK...

THEN--MY FUMBLING FINGERS CLOSED AROUND THE *T.N.T.*, AND I FLIPPERED OFF...

WHEN IS HE GOING TO GO FOR ME... WHEN... WHEN--?

IT SEEMED TO TAKE A MILLION YEARS BEFORE I COULD PLANT THE *T.N.T.* ON THE SUB... AND THEN.. AS I TURNED AWAY...

ENEMY FISHMEN!-- GOT TO KEEP THEM FROM SPOTTING THE *T.N.T.*!

I TORE INTO THE ENEMY FROGMEN...

GOT TO HOLD 'EM OFF--!

TRYING TO BLOCK OFF THE T.N.T. FROM THEM...

HOLD 'EM--!

BEFORE THEY COULD RIP IT OFF...

HOLD 'EM--!

THEN--TIME RAN OUT FOR THE T.N.T. AND THE SUB... AND WE WERE ALL TOSSED SKYWARDS.

HROOM

MY AIR HOSE WAS RIPPED BY THE EXPLOSION AND MY SHOULDERS WERE SO WRENCHED THAT...

HOPE THE PICKUP BOAT'S AROUND-- I'M PARALYZED!

AS I POPPED OUT ONTO THE SURFACE... THERE WAS A RECEPTION COMMITTEE OF TWO-- WAITING FOR ME...

ENEMY FROGMEN!-- CAN'T MOVE MY ARMS--! LOOKS LIKE THE END OF THE LINE FOR ME!

SUDDENLY, A DARK FIGURE KNIFED THROUGH THE WATER--AND RAMMED INTO THE ENEMY LIKE A LOCOMOTIVE...

IT'S-- THE SHARK!

THUUDD--!

IN A MOMENT I WAS ALONE...

HE'S FINALLY ATTACKING... I'M NEXT--!

I SAW HIS FIN COMING TOWARDS ME...

I DON'T KNOW WHAT MADE ME DUCK **UNDER** THE WATER...

HE'S PASSING... RIGHT... BY... ME--!

AS I WATCHED HIM BULLET INTO THE DISTANCE...

I HAVE THE FEELING THAT AS LONG AS I WAS **UNDERWATER**-- HE THOUGHT I WAS JUST ANOTHER **FISH**--AND LET ME ALONE... BUT I'LL NEVER BE ABLE TO PROVE IT... WITHOUT ASKING HIM!

the END

I'M SGT. ROCK OF EASY COMPANY...

--AND THE BIGGEST LAUGH IN THE OUTFIT IS *WHY* IT WAS CALLED *EASY!*

TAKE THE TIME WE SAW THE *EIGHTY-EIGHTS* "MARCHIN'" UP THE ROAD TOWARDS US WITH *T.N.T* STEPS...

INTO THAT SHELL-HOLE! THAT OLD ONE THERE--! *HOP! SKIP! JUMP!*

WHAM!

BLAM!

WHAM!

WE TUMBLED INTO THAT HOLE AS IF WE WERE *G.I. TENPINS* KNOCKED OVER BY A GIANT BOWLIN' BALL...

WHAM!

BAM!

PULL IN YOUR BELTS-- MAKE ROOM FOR EVERYBODY!

WE WERE PINNED DOWN LIKE FLAP-JACKS ON A HOT GRIDDLE... AND AS I LOOKED AROUND...

WHAM!

WHAM!

WHAM!

THIS BETTER NOT LAST TOO LONG! NOTHIN' RATTLES GUYS SO MUCH LIKE BEIN' ON A *BULL'S-EYE!*

SUDDENLY, THE BUILT-IN "ALARM" I HAD FROM YEARS OF COMBAT--BEGAN RINGIN' IN MY HEAD...

MOVE OUT! TAKE OFF! GET OUT OF HERE! PULL OUT THE STOPS!

THE GUYS MUST'VE THOUGHT I WAS OFF MY ROCKER...

SARGE! YOU WANT US TO CATCH THOSE *EIGHTY-EIGHTS* IN OUR TIN POTS?

WE'RE HOPPIN' OUT'VE THE ENEMY FRYIN' PAN--INTO THE FIRE!

GO!-- GO! GO!

BLAM!

BAM!

WHAM!

BEIN' MEN FROM EASY-- THEY BEEFED-- BUT FOLLOWED ME...

INTO THIS *NEW* SHELL-HOLE HERE!

ROCK'S TAKIN' US ON A GUIDED TOUR!

WHAT'S THE MATTER, *ROCK?* DIDN'T YOU LIKE OUR *OLD* "APARTMENT"?

THAT'S *JUST* IT, NICK! IT WAS *TOO OLD!*

AND AS THEY PEERED OVER OUR HOLE, THEY SAW THE WARNIN' THAT HAD BUZZED AROUND IN MY TIN POT A COUPLE OF SECONDS AGO...

A DIRECT HIT! AS IF THOSE ENEMY GUNNERS KNEW *EXACTLY* WHERE THAT SHELL HOLE WAS!

YEAH--AN' WAITED UNTIL THEIR SHELLIN' WOULD DRIVE US *INTO* IT FOR SHELTER!

AS THE SHELLIN' BEGAN LOOKIN' FOR US AGAIN...

WONDER WHAT THOSE JOKERS WILL THINK UP NEXT, ROCK?

THAT'S EASY! THEY'LL KEEP US PINNED DOWN--AN' WAIT UNTIL WE JUMP UP AN' RUN RIGHT INTO THEIR SIGHTS!

THE ENEMY HAD PLENTY OF AMMO... AND SPREAD IT AROUND--PRACTICALLY RIGHT OVER OUR TIN POTS UNTIL THE THING I WAS HOPIN' *WOULDN'T* HAPPEN--*DID*...

LEMME OUT! LEMME GET ONE SHOT AT THOSE GUYS -- JUST ONE SHOT--*ONE SHOT!*

105

THERE'S ONLY ONE WAY TO STOP A GUY FROM BLOWIN' HIS STACK -- *GRAB HIM !*

ALL IT TAKES IS ONE GUY TO START A SUBWAY RUSH HOUR INTO THE ENEMY GUNS -- AND IT'S NOT GOIN' TO HAPPEN TO *EASY !*

I HELD THE GUY DOWN UNTIL HE CAME TO... AND THEN STARTED THE OLDEST GIMMICK IN THE WORLD TO KEEP EVERYONE'S ATTENTION AWAY FROM THE FIREWORKS GOIN' ON ALL AROUND US...

YOU THINK *YOU'RE* THE ONLY GUYS WHO WERE IN A SPOT WHERE YOU *COULDN'T FIRE A SHOT ?*

I COULD SEE THAT THEY HAD *ONE* EAR LISTENIN' TO ME -- AND THE *OTHER* ON THE SHELLS... BUT AT LEAST -- THAT WAS A BEGINNIN'...

TAKE OUR FIRST BEACH PARTY... WE HAD GONE DOWN THE NETS... AND STARTED ON OUR RIDE TO THE BEACH WHEN ...

" WE GOT TAGGED BY AN ENEMY SHORE BATTERY ! "

BLANG!

" I TRIED TO COUNT TIN POTS WHEN WE REACHED THE SURFACE ... "

EVERYONE'S HERE -- BUT LARRY ! WELL -- HOPE WE'LL MEET HIM ASHORE ! *LET'S GO, EASY !*

" WE COULDN'T FIRE BACK AT THE LEAD THAT WAS DROPPIN' ALL AROUND US LIKE RAIN -- *AND SWIM* -- SO WE HEADED FOR SHORE *WITHOUT FIRIN' A SHOT !* "

WONDER WHAT HAPPENED TO LARRY ?

As we found out later, LARRY had been tossed far out of the boat and had already **MET** the enemy--**WITHOUT FIRIN'** a shot either!"

FROGMAN!

"THE ENEMY FROGMAN thought he'd KAYOED LARRY--but he didn't know he was from **EASY**..."

HE'S SWIMMING TOWARD THOSE BOOBY TRAPS!

"IT DIDN'T TAKE A SECOND for LARRY to thresh his way towards that FROGMAN..."

HE'S GOING TO BLOW UP THOSE BOOBY TRAPS RIGHT IN **EASY'S** FACE!

"THERE WERE NO SHOTS FIRED as LARRY BULLETED INTO THE FROGMAN..."

GOT TO STOP HIM!

"A G.I. AIN'T supposed to be equipped with GILLS..."

CAN'T SHAKE HIM LOOSE FROM THE DETONATOR!

"BUT **EASY** GUYS..."

GOT TO MAKE HIM SET OFF THOSE BOOBY TRAPS--

"...CAN FIGHT ANYWHERE--EVEN UNDER WATER!"

--BEFORE THE GUYS REACH 'EM!

"THAT'S WHEN WE SAW THE WATER SOMERSAULT IN FRONT OF US LIKE A LINE OF T.N.T. ACROBATS..."

WE COULD'VE BEEN STEPPIN' RIGHT **OVER** THOSE!

WONDER WHO TRIGGERED 'EM **AHEAD** OF TIME?

BLAM! WHAM! BLAM! BLAM!

"THE ANSWER BOBBED UP RIGHT AHEAD OF US!"

IT'S LARRY!

LOOKS LIKE HE **ALREADY** FOUGHT THIS WAR! WE'VE GOT TO PASS HIM ON TO THE CORPSMEN!

I'M OUT'VE ACTION-- WITHOUT FIRING A SHOT, **ROCK**-- I CAN'T GO ON WITH **EASY!**

IF IT HADN'T BEEN FOR THE WAR **YOU** FOUGHT **WITHOUT** FIRIN' A SHOT, LARRY-- **EASY** WOULD'VE BEEN OUT OF ACTION!

AS I FINISHED--I COULD SEE THE GUYS' ATTENTION ON ME ... LIKE ANTENNA POINTIN' IN MY DIRECTION ...

SO YOU SEE? THIS AIN'T THE FIRST TIME **EASY'S** BEEN IN A SPOT WHERE YOU **COULDN'T** FIRE BACK!

YEAH--SARGE--YEAH! BUT WAS IT AS TOUGH AS ... THIS?

WHAM!

I WAS ABOUT TO SAY IT WAS TOUGHER--WHEN A BRACE OF SHELLS LANDED SO CLOSE THE BLAST KNOCKED MY TIN POT OFF...

BLAM!

WHILE THE BLAST WAS STILL RINGIN' LIKE A SEVEN DAY CLOCK IN MY EARS, I FELT THE GUY UNCOIL AGAINST ME LIKE A SPRING...

LEMME OUT! LEMME GET A SHOT AT 'EM! I'M NOT GOIN' TO BE TRAPPED IN HERE-- WITHOUT FIRIN' A SHOT BACK!

I PUSHED HIM BACK... AND FUMBLED FOR MY TIN POT MAKIN' BELIEVE IT DIDN'T LOOK A MILE AWAY...

THIS JUMPIN' JACK UNDER ME IS **THE** KEY!

I MADE BELIEVE LIKE MY TIN POT DIDN'T FEEL LIKE IT WEIGHED A TON AS I LIFTED IT BACK ON.. HIDIN' MY OWN SHAKES...

IF I CAN KEEP **HIM** FROM FLIPPIN' HIS LID--THE REST OF THE GUYS 'LL BE CALM!

SO I BEGAN AGAIN...

AFTER WE LEFT LARRY WITH THE MEDICS ...WE PUSHED ON OFF THE BEACH THROUGH WOODS THICKER THAN THE SUNDAY PAPERS!

"SUDDENLY, A MACHINE GUN OPENED UP ON US LIKE A BANK THAT HADN'T HAD A CUSTOMER IN YEARS--ONLY IT WAS HANDIN' OUT LEAD-- NOT DOLLAR BILLS!"

START PLOUGHIN' FARMERS!

VIIP! ZIIP! VIIP!

"WE DIDN'T KNOW WHERE THAT MG WAS FIRIN' FROM--BUT--WE HAD WALKED RIGHT INTO ITS FIRE LANE...AND ALL IT HAD TO DO WAS FIRE BLIND--TO GET US ALL...SOONER OR LATER..."

WE'LL NEVER FIND IT WITH OUR TIN POTS IN THE DIRT!

YEAH--LET'S TRY LIFTIN' OURS!

ZIIP! VIIP! BWEE!

"WE LIFTED OUR HELMETS ON THE ENDS OF OUR RIFLES--JUST FOR A TEST--"

"THE NEXT SECOND--THEY RANG LIKE MIDGET BOILER FACTORIES!"

SPLANG!

ZIING!

SPLANG!

"STEVE DROPPED HIS RIFLE.. AND CHECKED HIS GRENADES..."

GIVE ME ALL THE FIRE YOU CAN, SARGE!

NOT KNOWIN' WHERE THE GUN IS--ALL WE CAN GIVE YOU IS HARASSIN' FIRE!

"AT MY YELL--ALL THE GUYS BEGAN FIRIN' AHEAD OF THEM BLINDLY-- INTO THE WALL OF UNDERBRUSH..."

RAPID FIRE! THROW LEAD AROUND--!

WHERE, SARGE?

BUDDA!

POW! POW!

"WHAT COULD I TELL THEM? I WAS AS BLIND AS THEY WERE!"

YOU'VE GOT A NOSE, AIN'T YOU? FOLLOW IT!

BUDDA!

POW!

"IN THE MIDST OF OUR BLIND CRAZY FIRIN', I LOOKED FOR STEVE..."

HE'S GONE!

"LATER WE LEARNED THAT STEVE HAD MONKEYED UP THE NEAREST TREE..."

FIRING'S COMING FROM THERE!

RATATAT!

"STEVE DIDN'T EVEN TRY TO DUCK THE LEAD FLYIN' AROUND WILDLY... HE MOVED FROM TREE TO TREE... HOLDIN' HIS BREATH... FIGHTIN' A WAR WITHOUT FIRIN' A SHOT!"

IT MIGHT BE DOWN THERE! SOUNDS LIKE IT! BUT THE WOODS ARE FULL OF ECHOES! I MIGHT BE FOOLED! IF I DROP AN EGG--AND IT'S IN THE WRONG PLACE--THEY'LL SPRAY UP AND GET ME!

RATATAT!

"STEVE SHINNIED DOWN AS LOW AS HE COULD IN THAT CHOKIN' FOLIAGE..."

WELL-- I'VE GOT A COUPLE OF HOT POTATOES IN MY MITTS NOW! I'LL HAVE TO CARRY 'EM THE REST OF THE WAY!

"HE CAME DOWN LIKE A PANCAKIN' STUKA--RIGHT ON THE ENEMY GUNNERS!"

"IT WAS A QUESTION OF WHO WOULD SUCK THEIR WIND BACK FIRST-- STEVE OR THE GUNNERS.."

CAN'T--LET-- GO--OF-- GRENADES!

THEY'LL GO OFF--THE SECOND...

I--LET GO!

"*THAT TANK HAD US BUT GOOD--AND AS IT OPENED UP ON US...*"

FLOP **ON** THE ROAD-- OR YOU'LL LAND ON THE **BOOBY TRAPS!**

"*WE HAD ONE BREAK--I ALWAYS HAD VIC, THE BAZOOKAMAN UP FRONT--IN CASE WE RAN INTO SOMETHIN' LIKE THIS--AND HE WAS IN A PERFECT SPOT TO MAKE A KILL...*"

ONE--TWO-- THREE--AND AWAY YOU G--

"*VIC DIDN'T HAVE A CHANCE TO FINISH-- BECAUSE THE TANK STARTED RHYMIN' IN LEAD...*"

RA-TA-TA-TAT!

"*SO WHILE THE TANK PINNED US DOWN... SO WE COULDN'T FIRE A SHOT... WE WATCHED IT GRIND ON...RIGHT OVER THE BAZOOKA!*"

GRNNG!

"*WE HAD NOTHIN' NOW--TO FIGHT THAT TANK WITH--EXCEPT MAYBE OUR DOGTAGS...AND THEN AS I EDGED BACK...*"

ANTI-TANK MINE--MIGHT'VE LOST MY DOGTAGS IF I HIT IT HARD ENOUGH!

THUD!

"I WASN'T THE ONLY GUY THAT MUST'VE TRIED TO SHUFFLE BACK OUT OF THE LEAD RAIN THE TANK WAS TOSSIN' OUT--AND KNOCKED AGAINST ONE OF THE MINES AT THE SIDE OF THE ROAD.. BECAUSE..."

LOOK AT THAT DOGFACE-- PUSHIN' THAT MINE AHEAD OF HIM!

HE'S TRYIN' TO MAKE THAT SHELL HOLE TO OPERATE FROM!

"IF THAT *G.I.* HAD HOPES OF GETTIN' *INTO* THAT HOLE AND STAY *IN*, WHILE HE PUSHED THE MINE OUT *UNDER* THE TANK--THE TANK GUNNERS SOON STOPPED HIM..."

KAPUT!

RA-TAT!

"BUT IT'S NOT SO EASY TO RUBBERSTAMP *KAPUT* ON A GUY FROM *EASY* EVEN IF HE WAS FIGHTIN' A WAR WITHOUT FIRIN' A SHOT!"

GOT TO ROLL OUT'VE THE WAY OF THE TANK AT THE LAST MOMENT...OR IT'LL TURN *AWAY* FROM THIS *BOOBY TRAP!*

MY BODY'S HIDIN' THIS MINE--

"THE TREADS WERE SO CLOSE, THE CREW COULDN'T SEE THE GUY FROM *EASY* ROLL OUT OF THE WAY..."

WILL THIS RING UP THE CASH REGISTER?

"IT DID..."

BLANG!

114

HERE'S ANOTHER TALE OF THE COMBAT-HAPPY JOES OF EASY COMPANY--AS TOLD UNDER FIRE BY THE ROCK OF EASY, SGT. ROCK! BUT LET HIM TELL IT TO YOU IN HIS OWN WORDS--EXACTLY HOW IT HAPPENED! IN...
3 STRIPES HILL!
SPANG
COME IN, EASY! COME IN! ARE YOU HOLDING?
WE'RE STILL HOLDIN'! EASY'S STILL HOLDIN'!
POW
KPOW
POW
ZIP
ZIP
ZING
TZING
JOE KUBERT

I'M SGT. ROCK OF EASY COMPANY... I WAS CHECKIN' POST NO. 3 FOR THE NIGHT WHEN...

THERE GOES THE ROCK ON HIS ROUNDS!

HE LOOKS LIKE HE WAS *BORN* WITH THOSE *THREE STRIPES!*

THE GUNNERS DIDN'T KNOW I HEARD 'EM...

I DIDN'T *ALWAYS* HAVE THESE *THREE STRIPES!* IN FACT, THERE WAS A LONG TIME WHEN IT DIDN'T SEEM I'D EVER HAVE *ONE*--LET ALONE *THREE!*

I WOULDN'T WANT TO EARN THESE STRIPES *AGAIN*-- THE *WAY* I HAD TO! I'D RATHER DO WITHOUT 'EM! AND SPEND THE REST OF THIS WAR WITH A CLEAN SLEEVE! IF I HAD A CHOICE--BUT I *DIDN'T* HAVE A CHOICE...

IT ALL STARTED A LONG TIME AGO... WHEN *EASY* COMPANY WAS AS *GREEN* AS A DOLLAR BILL JUST COME OUT'VE THE MINT... AND I WAS A BUCK PRIVATE IN THE OUTFIT!

"I WAS WITH A BUDDY OF MINE, NICK BARTON... WE WERE IN A TRUCK WITH OTHER *EASY* GUYS ON THE WAY TO THE FRONT..."

THAT SLEEVE WON'T BE SO *BARE* AFTER THIS ATTACK, *ROCK!* AND NEITHER WILL *MINE!* SAY-- HOW ABOUT MAKIN' *BOOK* AS TO *WHO* COLLECTS *MORE* STRIPES?

"JUST THEN--SOMEONE ELSE ENTERED A BET OF HIS OWN-- A STUKA PILOT..."

SKREEEEEE

RATATAT

RATAT

"WHEN WE REACHED THE JUMPIN'-OFF PLACE FOR THE ATTACK...A LOW HILL FACIN' A RIVER...THE CAPTAIN SPOKE TO ME ... "

ROCK--I'M PUTTING YOU IN FOR A BRONZE STAR! YOU SHOULD GET A COUPLE OF STRIPES FOR WHAT YOU DID! BUT THE COMPANY TABLE OF ORGANIZATION IS FILLED! THE ONLY WAY THE LIEUTENANT HERE CAN BECOME CAPTAIN-- IS IF THE ENEMY RETIRES ME !

AND THE SERGEANT HERE CAN'T GET A BATTLEFIELD PROMOTION TO LIEUTENANT--UNLESS AN ENEMY SLUG DETOURS ME !

" THEY WERE KIDDIN'-- THE WAY BRAVE MEN KID ABOUT THINGS THEY'RE AFRAID OF... "

I'M SATISFIED WITH THE COMPANY T.O. THE WAY IT IS, SIR ! I DON'T WANT TO JUMP OVER ANYONE TO GET A STRIPE ! AS FOR THE STAR ...THANKS, SIR ... BUT NICK WOULD HAVE GOTTEN IT ... IF HE'D REACHED ...THE GUN--

"THEN, IT WAS TIME...AND WE STARTED DOWN THE HILL TOWARDS THE RIVER...I WAS WITH THREE OTHER MEN...AND BECAUSE THE QUIET FELT LIKE A DAGGER AT OUR THROATS...THEY BEGAN KIDDIN' ME."

IF I'M STOPPED-- THE CORPORAL WILL GET MY STRIPE !

AND IF I GET STUNG BY A BEE--FIRST CLASS WILL GET MINE !

ROCK'S HELMET IS BARE AS A BILLIARD BALL ! IF HE'S THE ONLY ONE TO GET ACROSS THE RIVER-- HE'LL GET ALL OUR STRIPES !

"THE ENEMY WAITED 'TIL EASY WAS DOWN THE HILL AND FACIN' THE RIVER WHEN THEY BEGAN DUMPIN' MORTARS DOWN ON US..."

WE CAN'T GO BACK ! THERE WOULDN'T BE ENOUGH GUYS LEFT TO FORM A SQUAD-- BEFORE WE COULD CLIMB BACK UP THE HILL !

VROOSH

WHUMP

"THE ENEMY MORTAR CREWS WERE SMART COOKIES..."

WHUMP WHUMP WHUMP WHUMP WHUMP

WHUMP WHUMP

WHUMP

BLAM

WHAAM

BLAM

THEY GAVE US THE CHOICE OF BEIN' CLOBBERED TRYIN' TO GET **BACK** UP THE HILL-- OR TRYIN' TO OUTRUN THE MORTAR SHELLS-- **ACROSS THE RIVER!**

WE WERE **OUT** OF MORTAR RANGE WHEN WE WERE **IN** THE RIVER --BUT NOW WE WERE RIGHT IN THE FIRE LANES OF ENEMY PILLBOX MACHINE GUNS -- THIS WAS **JUST** WHAT THEY WERE **WAITIN'** FOR ...

RATATAT

"**WE** COULDN'T GO BACK-- AND WE COULDN'T **STAY** WHERE WE WERE ..."

SOME FUN!

THAT'S **EASY** FOR YOU! WHERE THE FIGHTIN'S **NEVER** EASY!

TZING

ZIP ZIP

ZIP

FLUP

"YOU CAN CALL THE INFANTRY 'FLAT-FOOT' OR 'DOUGH-FOOT'--ONE THING'S SURE--IT'S NOT 'WEB-FOOT'--

IF THEY KEEP ON DUMPIN' IN ANY MORE LEAD--THEY'LL RAISE THE LEVEL OF THE WATER ABOVE MY TIN POT--AND DROWN ME!

IF THE COMPANY T.O. WASN'T FILLED, ROCK-- YOU'D MAKE SERGEANT ON LAUGHS ALONE!

YEAH, SARGE? ROCK COULD HAVE MY STRIPES--IF I COULD GET A TRANSFER STARTIN' NOW!

VIP VIP

BEEOW

TLING   ZIP   ZIP

"THERE AIN'T NO FANCY WAY TO CROSS A RIVER UNDER FIRE-- YOU JUST HOPE NO ONE'S SIGHTIN' IN ON YOUR DOGTAGS--AND KEEP ON GOIN' !"

TZING

VIP

BWEEOW

TZINNG   VIP

"I WAS SO MAD AT THE TRAP WE'D WALKED INTO THAT I SCRAMBLED FOR THE PILLBOX AS IF IT WAS HANDIN' OUT RAFFLES FOR A TURKEY !"

ZIP   Z'ING   ZIP   VIP

"BUT IF THEY WERE HANDIN' OUT RAFFLES FOR A TURKEY--THEIR SLUGS SHOWED ME THAT I WAS THE TURKEY !"

RATATATAT

"WHEN MY TIN POT STOPPED SOUNDIN' LIKE A BOILER FACTORY ON DOUBLE TIME..."

THEY THINK THEY'VE COOKED *THIS* TURKEY!

RATATAT

"I HEATED UP A GRENADE WHILE THEY WERE FIRIN' OVER ME AT THE OTHER GUYS STILL COMIN' OUT OF THE RIVER..."

PLING

RAT ATA

HATCH!

"I ROLLED OUT OF THE WAY OF THE MACHINE GUN SWIVEL'IN' DOWN TOWARDS ME..."

RATATAT

ZING ZIP

VIP

LOOKS LIKE I HATCHED A SOFT-BOILED EGG!

"BUT THE NEXT SECOND PROVED THE EGG WAS HARD-BOILED ENOUGH TO CRACK THE PILLBOX WIDE OPEN!"

BLAM

"*WHO* DO YOU THINK HELPED ME UP?--"

GREAT WORK, *ROCK*! WE ALL SAW IT-- AND WE'RE ALL REPORTIN' IT TO THE *C.O.*!

"AND *WHAT* DO YOU THINK THE *C.O.* TOLD ME?"

LOOKS LIKE YOU'LL GET ANOTHER *STAR* OUT OF THIS, *ROCK*! BUT, I *CAN'T* GET YOU A *STRIPE*! THE *COMPANY'S T.O.* IS ALL FILLED!

IT'S *O.K.* WITH ME, SIR! I'M *NOT* BUCKIN' FOR *STRIPES* OVER ANOTHER GUY'S TIN POT STUCK ON A RIFLE!

"YEAH--**EASY** GOT ACROSS THE RIVER--BUT IT **COST!**"

YOU CAN'T CROSS A RIVER--WITHOUT SOMEONE GETTIN' HIS FEET WET!

"THE FOUR OF US MADE A **TEAM**... THE **SARGE**, THE **CORP**, THE **FIRST CLASS** AND ME, THE **BUCK PRIVATE**..."

WAITIN' FOR **MY** STRIPES, CORP?

I'M IN NO HURRY, SARGE--BUT THE **FIRST** IS FOR MY STRIPES!

NOT ME! ALL I FEEL IS **ROCK'S** HOT BREATH ON **MY** ONE STRIPE!

"THEN LIKE AN ACT, THEY WAITED FOR **ME** TO JUMP AT THE CUE AS IF I WAS A STRAIGHT MAN FOR A COMIC!"

KEEP YOUR TIN POTS ON YOUR HEADS--AND YOUR STRIPES ON YOUR SLEEVES--**I DON'T WANT 'EM!**

"IF A SNIPER OPENED UP ON THE SARGE..."

POW

"THAT WAS **HIS** FATAL MISTAKE--BECAUSE THE **CORP** ALWAYS COVERED THE SARGE..."

YOU'LL **NEVER** MAKE SERGEANT, CORPORAL--UNLESS YOU STOP RINGIN' UP THOSE BULL'S-EYES!

K-POW

"IF A POTATO MASHER TRIED TO TOSS THE **CORP** INTO THE NEXT LEAGUE..."

"THE FIRST-CLASS COVERED HIM SO FAST--THE POTATO MASHER WAS SLAMMED BACK TO ITS PITCHER FOR A LOUD STRIKE-OUT!"

YOU'LL **NEVER** MAKE CORPORAL, FIRST CLASS-- UNLESS YOU MISS **ONCE** IN A WHILE!

BLAM

"THE THREE OF 'EM WERE SO GOOD--I NEVER HAD **ANYTHIN'** TO DO..."

I DON'T KNOW WHY YOU GUYS WANT **ME** ALONG?

MAYBE YOU'LL MAKE SERGEANT ON **THIS** JOB, **ROCK**!

"WE ALL GOT A GOOD LAUGH AT THAT AS WE DUG IN AT THE TOP OF BALDY HILL..."

ANY SIGN OF ENEMY ACTIVITY IN THE VALLEY, EASY?

NOT A SIGN, SIR!

WE DON'T EXPECT 'EM TO START ANYTHING! BUT IF THEY DO--HOLD THE HILL UNTIL WE REINFORCE YOU! WE WANT 'EM TO THINK YOU FOUR ARE THEIR ONLY OPPOSITION-- UNTIL WE CAN JUMP 'EM!

EASY'LL HOLD, SIR!

"THE **MESSER** MUST'VE BEEN ON ITS WAY HOME WHEN IT WAS SIGNALLED TO MAKE ONE PASS AT US.."

RATATAT

"BUT ITS PASS WAS A GOOD ONE..."

WHAM

"WHEN BRAVE MEN DON'T WANT YOU TO KNOW WHAT THEY FEEL DEEP DOWN--THEY JOKE ABOUT IT..."

WELL, *ROCK!* THE *T.O.* HAS ROOM FOR A *FIRST CLASS!* YOU'VE MADE IT!

YOU'VE GOT YOURSELF A STRIPE, *ROCK!* WHICH IS MORE THAN I'LL EVER GET!

EASY--COME IN! EASY--ARE YOU STILL HOLDING?

WE'RE HOLDIN', SIR!

"THE ENEMY STARTED ATTACKIN' ON *MY* SIDE... I OPENED FIRE AND YELLED..."

LOOKS LIKE THEY'RE PUTTIN' ALL THEIR EGGS IN ONE BASKET-- THE ONE ON *MY* SIDE!

THEY'RE TOO TRICKY TO RISK THAT! COVER THE OTHER SIDE, *CORP!*

"JUST AS THE SARGE AND I ROLLED 'EM BACK ON *OUR* SIDE-- WE HEARD A MUFFLED EXPLOSION RIGHT *BEHIND* US..."

ZIP ZIP ZING ZIP ZIP

WHUMP

CORP--!

"THE ENEMY HAD SNEAKED A RIFLE GRENADIER THROUGH ON THE CORPORAL'S SIDE... HE HAD LANDED ONE IN OUR FOXHOLE ... AND THE CORP HAD COVERED US ..."

WELL, *ROCK!* YOU'RE MOVIN' UP! THE *T.O.'s* GOT ROOM FOR A *TWO-STRIPER*-- AND YOU'RE IT!

"WHEN THE *C.O.* CALLED UP TO FIND OUT WHAT THE SHOOTIN' WAS ABOUT."

EASY 2 *EASY?* YOU STILL HOLDING?

WE'RE STILL HOLDIN', SIR!

"WE BOTH SAW THE TANK AT THE SAME TIME.."

GOTTA STOP IT--BEFORE IT GETS UP HERE! COVER ME, ROCK! FILL THE VIEW SLITS WITH HOT LEAD SO I CAN GET CLOSE TO IT! THAT'S AN ORDER, ROCK! YOU STAY--I GO!

"I PUMPED LEAD AT THE SLITS AS FAST AS I COULD UNTIL MY GUN BARREL SIZZLED..."

THEY CAN'T SEE THE SARGE ATTACKIN' FROM THE SIDE! HE'S TRYIN' TO SET OFF THE AMMO!

KPOW POW POW

"HE DID!" BLANG

SARGE!

"WHEN I CARRIED HIM BACK, I REALIZED THAT THE SARGE HAD BEEN HIT ON HIS WAY TO THE TANK--BUT BEIN' AN EASY COMPANY SERGEANT-- HE JUST KEPT ON GOIN' UNTIL HE FINISHED HIS JOB!"

LOOKS LIKE...THE T.O.'LL HAVE ROOM...FOR A BRAND-NEW SERGEANT...AND YOU'VE EARNED...THE THIRD...STRIPE... SERGEANT ROCK...

"THE ENEMY STARTED ATTACKIN' BEHIND THE TANK--FIGURIN' THERE WAS NO ONE LEFT BY NOW..."

RATATATAT KPOW POW POW

"SO DID THE WALKIE-TALKIE..."

EASY?-- EASY? YOU STILL HOLDING? COME IN, EASY! COME IN!

"EASY-- EASY-- ARE YOU HOLDING?"

"WE ARE, SIR! AND WE'LL HOLD THE HILL UNTIL YOU COME UP!"

"BUT THE ENEMY WAS *WRONG*...AND SO WAS THE WALKIE-TALKIE..."

KPOW POW

BEEOW

TZING

ZIP

"THE ENEMY GOT THERE *FIRST*-- AND STAYED ABOUT THIRTY SECONDS... THE LONGEST HALF MINUTE IN MY LIFE..."

"BEFORE THE COMBAT-HAPPY JOES OF EASY COMPANY PUSHED 'EM BACK-- *ALL THE WAY BACK*..."

"OKAY, ROCK! SIMMER DOWN! LET THE COMPANY TAKE OVER NOW!"

BAM

YEAH-- IT ALL HAPPENED A LONG TIME AGO... A *LONG TIME AGO*... WHEN THE WAR AND *EASY CO.* WERE GREEN AS DOLLAR BILLS FROM THE MINT...

NO-- I WASN'T *BORN* WITH THESE *THREE STRIPES*...

I KEPT ON CHECKIN' THE MACHINE GUN POSTS FOR THE NIGHT...

IT AIN'T EASY BEIN' A SERGEANT-- ESPECIALLY IN EASY COMPANY!

The End